TWISTED TRUTHS

P. RAYNE

About Twisted Truths

My life changed forever the day I saved Obsidian Voss from drowning in the ocean.

When my father lands himself in trouble, I take a job working for Obsidian, one of the country's most famous billionaires. It doesn't take long for me to realize that there's more behind the façade he presents to the world—a darker, more dangerous side.

Still, I'm drawn to him. As he introduces me to a world I never knew existed, I find myself falling for him. But I'm torn because I came to Midnight Manor with a hidden agenda, and I've been lying to Obsidian from the start. Eventually, he's going to find out.

My secret will change everything. And if Obsidian really is the monster he thinks he is, what will he do to me?

the Midnight Manor series

TWISTED TRUTHS

P. RAYNE

TRIGGER WARNINGS

Trigger warnings can be found on our website if you want
to check them out.

PLEASE NOTE:
These warnings contain major spoilers.

https://piperrayne.com/midnight-manor

Playlist

Here's a list of songs that inspired us while we were writing the Midnight Manor series. You can follow the playlist (and us) on Spotify using the QR code below.

CHAPTER

ONE

I'm not even sure why the fuck I'm here.

I toss back the remainder of my drink and rest the glass on the railing of the deck. For the past couple of weeks, I've been holed up in a small cabin on the West Coast.

I scratch at the short beard I've grown—an attempt to remain anonymous in my travels, along with leaving my cell phone at home and only using cash so my brothers can't track me.

The desire to leave my home and my brothers boiled higher every day until it bubbled over, and I fled our mansion. Anabelle moving in was the first simmer. Her living with us changed everything at Midnight Manor. Then came Rapsody, and the pressure grew intense, but I held on knowing my brothers needed me. Ultimately, Cinder broke me.

One by one, my brothers found someone to share their hearts, lives, and love with. God, I could choke just thinking of that word. *Love.* Never would I have thought that my brothers had it in them to love anyone but themselves. We weren't brought up to believe in anything other than survival.

Then again, none of them are as fucked in the head as me. Courtesy of our good ol' dad. May he rest in the fiery coals of hell for all eternity.

No one was more surprised than me when these feelings crept up. Why the hell should I care if my brothers are now in love? But as each woman moved in and my brother's dining room chairs became vacant for our breakfasts and dinners, I felt like a flower people were pulling petals off of one by one, and pretty soon I'll be just a bare stem.

With a sigh, I step back to sit my ass in the chair, but I stagger, grabbing the armrest, and ease into the chair. A sign I should've eaten dinner before starting in with the booze—again. But that's how I've spent these weeks—drinking and smoking myself into oblivion. Anything to escape the swirling thoughts of the past and a bleak and solitary future.

It feels so good to give into my basest self and not have to put up the front of a charming, debonair billionaire who has nothing to hide.

It would be like finding gold at the bottom of the ocean if I found someone who understands my proclivities. Who won't judge me. Won't judge my past and will find me worthy.

Which is all kinds of fucked up because never once in my life, not for one second, have I ever thought I'd ride off into the sunset with someone. Never wanted to. Still don't.

But now that my brothers have settled down, it's like I don't fit anymore. At one time, we were the mysterious, tortured Voss brothers with a fucked-up past, but now... now I don't know what we are—or more importantly, what I am.

Well, I know what I am—alone. And maybe that's it. Maybe I've realized that's my greatest fear. Because while my brothers are living their lives with someone who understands them, forgives them, I'm here—alone.

Just as my father predicted.

Dark clouds settle over the raging ocean. The salty air whips over the rippling water and rattles the paint-chipped shutters of the cabin.

Another storm is brewing. You'd think the weather would be better in June. I probably brought the shit weather with me. I'm like *Charlie Brown*, traveling around with a rain cloud over his head.

The white caps in the ocean call my name, beckoning me to join them. I manage to stand, barely keeping my balance. For the past week, I've been learning to surf, and I never expected it to be so addictive. It's as if I'm one and the same as the ocean—ominous and menacing. The breeze grows colder as I pick up my surfboard and trek down the beach, heading toward the water.

I'm not nearly experienced enough to be out there with the thunderous waves.

But maybe that's the point. To feel powerless, overtaken by something bigger than myself.

As my foot steps into the water, acceptance coats my skin like a wetsuit. Relief floods through me.

Other surfers are dotted along the canopy of the gray sea, far enough out to avoid the jagged rocks that peek out every so often in the lull between waves. I lie on my surfboard, paddling out, and by the time I reach my destination, my arms weigh heavily, likely from dehydration and hunger. I sit atop my surfboard, bobbing up and down with each wave, watching the other surfers meticulously pick waves and ride them toward the shore.

Who would think of surfing as a war? Each man trying to conquer nature, and nature fighting back. People in the water cheer with each successful ride, but I watch solemnly, keenly aware of the dark aching pit in my soul that's growing larger by the day.

In truth, the ache has probably been stealthily consuming me since I was a child. Every false smile, every witty remark over the years, to patch up the damage. Until there was only crumbling plaster that fell away and revealed what had been there all along—darkness rotting.

All the other surfers look at the horizon, each of them razzing another surfer to go after the biggest wave barreling toward us. In a split-second decision, I gather the courage to do what I came out here to do.

Turning, I paddle and paddle then hop to my feet, standing on my board. I'm sure I don't look nearly as good as the experienced surfers, but I'm standing, aren't I?

People shout behind me, and I make too quick of a move, getting too high on the lip of the wave. The power flips me over, my head racing toward the sandy bottom. My surfboard flicks up behind me and slams into the back of my head.

The water moves me like a rag doll, the current sweeping me one way and then the next. Instead of fighting, I succumb to the ocean's force, allowing the water to control me and move me.

The sea pulls me under, and I give in to her demands. As I sink down to the depths of the unknown, peace surrounds me for the first time in my life. I smile as the light from above grows dimmer and dimmer while I fade into darkness.

CHAPTER
TWO

ARIANA

My board is tucked under my arm, my feet in the sandy ocean bottom, when I spot a man who has no business surfing in this weather. He flips off his board, getting bashed in the head with it, then the wave topples over him. My stomach plummets, and I wait for him to surface, but seconds tick by, and his head doesn't pop up to the surface.

Shit.

Fellow surfers shout to each other, but they'll never reach him in time. I'm the closest, so I ditch my surfboard, quickly tug off the ankle strap, and swim in a sprint to the spot where I saw him go down.

If I find him, it will be a small miracle. The current most likely dragged his body. When I think I'm close to the right spot, I dive. The saltwater stings my eyes, but only a bit. My eyes have grown used to it from years in the ocean. Out of all the places I've lived, the ocean is the only place I can clear my head.

I frantically circle, not finding any sign of his body, until my lungs burn, and I have no choice but to resurface. I take a quick breath and dive back under. It's dark, and the current tugs my body in different directions, but a flash of white catches my eye.

There.

I use all my strength, kicking and pulling my body down farther. Catching his hand, I tug him, swimming with the last of my strength to the surface, pulling his head above water and dragging his back to my front. I band one arm around him and swim toward shore.

He's unconscious, which honestly is probably better. In my years as a lifeguard, I've experienced near-drowning victims firsthand, and they often panic and fight against the person saving them. This man is large and muscled. If he were to fight me off—or worse, use me as leverage to keep him above the water—there's a good chance I'd drown.

I'm panting when we reach the shore, but I take his wrists and drag him up onto the sand, just far enough that the waves don't fall over him. My chest heaves as I check for a pulse, not finding one.

"Damn it."

I straddle his waist and begin chest compressions, using all my might to push on his chest before I breathe air into his lungs. I hum the Bee Gees' song, "Staying Alive," which some might find ridiculous, but it's what I was taught because it has 103 beats per minute—the correct rate for doing chest compressions.

My voice grows labored as I sing when he doesn't come to after the first couple rounds.

I'm vaguely aware of people gathering around me, and I hear someone on the phone with 911, but my concentration doesn't break.

I alternate between compressions and mouth-to-mouth until I'm so exhausted I'm not sure how much longer I can continue. As if someone granted this man a miracle, he finally sputters and chokes up water.

I slide off of him, falling to my back, sucking air into my lungs. "Roll him on his side," I manage to say to one of the gawkers.

Coughing sounds next to me, which is a good sign. He's expelling his lungs, though he'll definitely need to make a trip to the hospital to be sure he doesn't succumb to secondary drowning.

Once my breathing stabilizes, the realization of what I just did sets in, as does the panic. I sit up and stagger onto my hands and knees, getting my bearings before I stand. I walk over to my bag I dropped down the beach, leaving my surfboard behind being beaten up in the ripples of waves at the shore.

"Hey!" someone calls after me, but I ignore them.

There's no way I'm going to be here when the ambulance and police show up. Even if I was a good Samaritan, I can't be on their radar—even for saving someone's life. My dad and brother would kill me.

And so, I leave the man behind, hoping I did enough to save him.

A COUPLE OF DAYS LATER, Bastion barges into my room without knocking.

My brother's not actually my brother by blood. My father took him in when he found Bastion as a runaway on the streets when he was eleven because Bastion was pickpocketing, and my dad thought he could be useful, which has proved right over the years.

I whip around from packing my change of clothes for my shift at the local bar. I'm scheduled to work tonight after I'm done with my regular job at the law office today.

"What the hell, Bast?" I narrow my blue eyes on his green ones.

"I should say the same to you." He tosses a folded newspaper onto the bed in front of me.

My forehead scrunches, and I pick up the paper, reading the headline of the article — "Mystery Woman Saves Billionaire from Drowning." *Billionaire?* Schooling my features, I drop the newspaper next to my bag.

"Why are you showing me this?" I neatly fold the T-shirt with the bar's name on it and place it in my bag, then shoulder the strap of my bag to face him.

He narrows his eyes. "You know exactly why."

"I don't." I try to move past him, but he steps in front of me.

"Cut the shit. I know it was you who rescued that guy."

I keep my features smooth, not about to give him the reaction he's searching for. "Oh?" Arching a brow, I continue. "Seems to me the headline reads mystery woman."

"Yeah, well, the article says it was a woman with long red hair and that it was a miracle she was able to drag him out of the ocean in that weather and administer CPR. I'm thinking that miracle happened because my little sis spent three years as a lifeguard at country clubs and is an adept swimmer."

I stare blankly at him. I shouldn't have to hide the fact I saved a man's life, but in this family, doing anything that might put a spotlight on you, good or bad, is seen as wrong.

"It could have been anyone." I shrug and shoulder past him.

"Maybe, but it was you. Ari, what were you thinking? You could've had the cops question you."

God, I'm so sick of this. This is exactly why six months ago, I told my dad and my brother that I wanted no part of their lifestyle.

I wheel around and face Bastion. "The guy was going to drown, and I was right there. What was I supposed to do? Swim past him and catch the next wave like a guy wasn't dying?"

"Yes! That's exactly what you should have done."

I narrow my eyes. Is he for real? "I guess that's where we're different then, Bast. Because I wouldn't swim past a drowning man, knowing I could help him."

Even if I have my own questions about whether he wanted to be saved or not. It was obvious he wasn't skilled enough to be out in the water in that weather, so I'm not sure why he was.

My brother shakes his head. "You're such a softie."

It used to drive me crazy when he referred to me as a softie. Back then, I was so focused on proving myself to him and my dad, it made me cave to whatever demands they made. But at twenty-four, I see it for what it is—a manipulation. A way for them to get me to put my conscience aside and do their bidding. Generally, something illegal or immoral and something that involves ripping someone off.

"Well, I guess that's why I left the family business then." I turn to leave before my dad catches wind of this conversation and finds out what I did.

From him, I'd get a lecture about how we can't do anything that draws any attention to us, especially from the cops. My dad would be concerned that the press might pick up the story and do some digging. And when you're grifters, that's not a good thing. The rule is to fly under the radar, move around a lot, don't make friends. Basically, be invisible. Oh, and to do what I'm told without exception.

"Ari, we can't let this just slip by us," Bast says before I reach the door.

So that's what this is really about. My brother can sniff out an opportunity from a mile away. He reads the word billionaire and automatically sees dollar signs.

With my hand on the knob of the front door, I turn to look

back at him. "I told you and Dad I was done with all that. I'm not interested."

Bast shakes his head for the thousandth time since he barged into my room. "So what, you're going to work a nine-to-five making shit money, find some boring schmuck to marry, and settle down? C'mon, you know that kind of life isn't for people like us. Or are you just gonna work two jobs for the rest of your life like you do now and put yourself in an early grave?"

I actually don't blame my brother for the way he thinks. He's a product of his environment, the same way I was. The day I finally worked up the courage to tell him and my dad that I was no longer going to participate in their scams was the hardest day of my life. I couldn't be sure they wouldn't kick me out because I'd no longer be useful to them. Sometimes I think my dad only lets me stay here because he thinks I'll change my mind.

"Don't worry about what I'm going to do. I'll be fine."

His lips turn down as if he pities me, and my hand tightens around the doorknob. "We're not done talking about this, Ari."

"We are."

The screen door slams shut behind me, and I walk quickly toward the bus stop. I had to sell my car a few months back when I could no longer afford it. Unfortunately, Bastion is right—a regular job doesn't pay nearly as well as crime.

But a clean conscience is worth having to use a bus pass. At least to me.

THREE

OBSIDIAN

A melody plays in my head in the voice of an angel. It takes me a moment to realize what keeps sounding on a loop in my head—a Bee Gees' song.

I blink my eyes open, squinting at the brazen overhead lights. It takes me a minute to realize I'm in a hospital bed —and not alone. My three brothers are huddled around me, their gazes filled with a mix of worry, relief, and fury.

"How did you find me?" My voice is raspy.

Kol takes pity on me and hands me a cup of water from the bedside table. I sit up and round my shoulders from the pain in my chest. "Someone recognized you and knew where you'd been staying. Found your wallet in that shack you were renting," he says as I swallow the entire cup of water in three gulps.

"What the fuck were you thinking?" Asher says because he's the oldest and took on the role of caregiver after our dad died.

"How are you feeling?" Nero asks, ever the peacemaker.

"Like I almost drowned." I tip up the corner of my lips, but it's clear that none of them will let me use charm to blow this off.

"What happened?" Kol asks seriously.

I shrug. "Apparently, I thought I was a better surfer than I was. Guess Mother Nature wins this round."

"You almost died," Asher seethes, his blue eyes boring into my near-black ones.

"Why didn't I?" I pass Kol the empty cup, and he refills it for me.

"Someone saved you. Pulled you from the water and gave you CPR."

My memory flits with a voice. That humming that's been in my head. "A woman..."

"Though no one seems to know who. She didn't stick around," Kol says and passes me another cup of water.

A gold locket with pearls along the chain. The image floats through my mind. The woman was wearing it, and it dangled in front of me when she was on top of me.

"Sid," Asher snaps.

I turn in his direction.

"Do you know who she was?" he asks.

I shake my head. "No idea."

Asher frowns. Maybe he wants to give her some reward money, but knowing Ash, he probably wants to check my story against hers.

"The important thing is that you're okay," Nero says.

The room is quiet for a beat before Kol asks, "Why'd you take off without telling anyone where you were going?"

Because I didn't want to have this conversation.

"Needed to clear my head." I down the water, my eyes focusing on the dry erase board in front of me with my name on it.

"That's all?" Asher says, and I look at him.

"That's all." Our gazes hold until he turns away.

"I'm going to call Anabelle and tell her he's okay," Asher says to Kol and Nero before leaving the room.

Nero's eyes shift between me and Kol, who is staring intently at me. "I'm gonna give Cinder a call too."

Kol's gaze flicks to Nero, and he nods. Once Nero leaves the room, Kol's jaw tightens. "So that's all it was... an accident?"

"What else would it be?" I hold his stare with my own. Daring him to say it. Daring him to accuse me of what he's assuming.

When he looks away, I know I've won this round.

Time to put the mask that I wear for the world back on, and

that weight buries me again. "You bring my phone with you?"

Kol nods and pushes his hand into his pocket, emerging with my phone fully charged.

"Thanks." I take it and pull up Mr. Smith's contact, typing out a text to him.

Got a job. Need you to find someone. Interested?

I set the phone face down on the bed beside me.

"Who are you texting?" Kol asks.

"Don't worry about it."

I want to find the woman who saved me. Although I'm not even sure why. Something in my gut tells me that I should.

WITHIN TWENTY-FOUR HOURS, my brothers have me on one of our private planes, whisking me back to Midnight Manor. I don't have the mental energy to fight them, so I go without protest.

No one questions me further on the way home. I almost think I've avoided any further backlash, until Asher sends me a text a few days later. Sometimes I'm jealous of his calculated patience.

Meet me in my office.

"Fuck," I grumble, pocketing my phone. He doesn't want to meet with me to see what work I'm behind on since my unannounced departure.

On the walk through Midnight Manor, I do my best to adopt an unaffected air, but it proves pointless because by the time I reach his office, I'm fixing for a fight like I am so often these days. It's becoming harder and harder to hide behind my mask.

The door is ajar when I arrive, and I stand on the threshold, finding all three of my brothers inside, stationed throughout the sitting area in front of the massive fireplace.

"To what do I owe the pleasure of this summoning?" I step inside and prowl over to an empty chair, undoing my suit jacket to sit.

"We've been talking, and we think it's time to make some changes around here." Asher starts, ever the eldest.

"What kind of changes?" I ask, interest piqued. There've been enough changes around this place now that all three of them have their significant others living in the manor.

"It dawned on me that the three of us have been preoccupied, and there's a possibility that left more work on your shoulders as far as Voss Enterprises is concerned."

Asher's not wrong, but I don't hate it. Now that they're coupled up for life, it's more obvious how very alone I am. But we're not here to talk about our feelings, so I'll take the win.

"I never said I minded." I shrug and rest my ankle on my knee.

"Regardless, we think it would be a good idea to hire someone to work by your side. Take some things off your plate and help you with whatever you need." Asher smooths his tie down his shirt, his eyes following his hand.

"I already have an assistant at the head office." My eyes narrow.

"True," Kol says. "But we think you could use someone here. Someone who would be here day in and day out. Someone who could anticipate your needs and step in before they become... overwhelming."

"Take some of the pressure off," Nero adds.

I scowl at the three of them. "Why does this feel like you're hiring a fucking babysitter for me?"

"That's not what this is," Kol insists, but they don't fool me.

They think what happened on the West Coast is a repeat of what happened a decade ago, but they're too chickenshit to come out and say it. So they want to hire someone to keep an eye on me.

I stand from the chair and button my suit jacket across my waist. "I don't need a snitch by my side day in and day out."

"Like Kol said, that's not what this is. You have a lot on your plate, a lot of moving parts. This person will just help you manage it, and they can do that most efficiently if they're here," Asher says.

"So what, they're going to live here?" I chuckle, but when they just stare at me, the laugh dies on my lips. "You can't be fucking serious."

"We think it's what's best—for you and for the company." Asher pins me with a stare, one I'm much too familiar with. It tells me that he's not going to back down.

I adjust my cufflinks, not looking at them. "Fine. You three do what you need to. As will I." Then I turn on my heel and stalk out of the office.

And what I'll do is make this person's life a living hell until they quit. And then the person after them and the one after them until my brothers figure out that I won't tolerate a babysitter.

FOUR

ARIANA

I only had a short shift at the bar tonight, so I step off the bus a little before ten o'clock and walk to our house. My late shifts are usually reserved for the nights I don't have to be up early to work at the law firm as a legal secretary.

I find my dad sitting on the couch, beer in hand, waiting for me. Otherwise, he wouldn't be here—he'd be off working some angle on someone somewhere. He always is. It's the one thing I can count on him for.

"Hi, Dad." I hang my bag and purse on the hook near the front door.

I grew up idolizing my father—he was my only parent since my mom ran off when I was five—but things have been tense between us since I told him I no longer want to take part in the family business.

"Ari." He nods and takes a pull from his beer. "How was work?"

"It was good. Where's Bast?"

"He's out with Katherine." A small smirk tilts the corner of his lips.

Katherine is Bast's latest mark. She's older, lonely, and wealthy, and when Bast turns on the charm toward a woman like that, she's putty in his hands.

"Cool, well, I'm going to hop in the shower and go to bed. I have to be up early."

I start toward the hallway, but my dad calls my name, and I stop in my tracks. I turn around slowly to face him. It's then I notice the same newspaper Bastion confronted me with this morning sitting on the coffee table.

"Bastion told you."

Asshole.

"Of course he did. *He's* loyal." Dad arches an eyebrow, and I blink back the sting in the corner of my eyes.

I know what I want for myself. I know that I'm on the right path, but it's still hard to set aside decades of indoctrination that make me feel as though I'm abandoning my family by turning my back on the grifter lifestyle.

My arms flail out at my sides. "I couldn't just let him drown."

"At least you got out of there before the cops came. What if this guy comes looking for you?"

My forehead wrinkles. "Why would he?"

"You saved a billionaire's life, Ari. Billionaire with a B. They live for being the center of attention and using the prose of rewarding their savior puts them in the spotlight."

I'm not going to tell my father that I'm pretty sure the guy had been trying to end his life, and there's just as good a chance that he'd be pissed at me for saving him. "That's not going to happen. He was barely even conscious when I left. He has no idea who I am."

He clucks his tongue. "Maybe you oughta think about telling him who you are."

I blink a few times. "My entire life, you've taught me to fly under the radar, and now you want me to poke my head out of the bunker waving a flag to draw attention?" I cross my arms.

He shrugs. "Maybe the reward outweighs the risk this time." He takes a pull off his beer until it's empty.

"I didn't save his life so I could get a reward from him. I didn't even know who he was when I saved him."

My dad smacks the empty bottle down on the worn coffee table and stands. "Ari, you're the one who got yourself into this situation, not me. But now that you're in it, you gotta play it for what it's worth, kid."

I shake my head. "I told you. I'm done with manipulating people and taking advantage of them."

"What manipulation? You saved the guy's life, didn't you? You deserve something for that."

"No, I don't." I start down the hallway toward my bedroom. "I just did what anyone would do."

"Do you have any idea what we could do with the amount of money a man like him could give you?" He follows me down the hall, stopping in the doorway.

"I'm not reaching out to him. Besides, there's no way to even prove it was me. There's probably a bunch of people coming out of the woodwork saying they're the ones who saved him for the exact reason you mention." I stand in front of my mirror and unbraid my long red hair so I can get into the shower.

"Hadn't thought of that." A quick glance at my dad lets me see the concern on his face. "Still worth a try though."

"No, it's not." I finger-comb my hair and turn back to the mirror.

"Ari, you gotta at least try. Where's the harm in that?"

It's the note of desperation in his tone that has me pause and slowly turn toward him. He hasn't fought me since my decision not to con anyone, so why is he being so persistent on this?

"What's going on?"

His face becomes a blank mask. "What do you mean? Nothing is going on."

My eyes narrow ever so slightly. "Are you sure?"

He scoffs. "'Course I'm sure. Just thought a windfall would be nice, that's all. But I can see that you still think you're too good for us. Still think you're better than us."

My shoulders sag. "You know it's not that. I just don't want to live my life ripping people off and constantly looking over my shoulder."

"Sure, Ari. Whatever you say." He stomps down the hall, and shortly after, the front door slams.

With a sigh, I make my way to the bathroom to shower.

Rather than relaxing like I want to, I spend the whole shower feeling guilty and second-guessing whether I should try contacting the man I saved. But I realize, despite the feeling of letting down my dad, I won't because that's not me anymore.

I didn't do it because I wanted his money, and I have no way to prove it was me anyway. And even more than that, I can't help but feel like in saving him, I was a part of something deeply personal and that he won't be thankful to me as my dad assumes.

I put it out of my mind as I get into my pajamas and dry my hair so I don't have to go to bed with it wet. When I'm finally finished and set the blow dryer down on the bathroom counter, I hear someone rustling around in the kitchen. The bungalow we rent isn't huge, so it doesn't take much commotion for me to overhear anything from the kitchen, but this is louder than normal.

Did my dad come back already?

I open the bathroom door, then hear, "Shit," and a moan.

Bastion.

Walking to the kitchen to investigate, I stop short when he whips around, a Ziploc bag filled with ice in his hand.

"What the hell happened?" My hand flies up to my mouth.

His face is covered in blood and bruises, and one of his eyes is almost swollen shut. He winces and walks with gentleness that says there are probably more bruises under his shirt.

My first thought is that maybe Katherine is a married woman, and her husband found out she's been sleeping with Bastion and buying him extravagant gifts. But the way Bast looks at me tells me that isn't it. He presses the ice to the corner of his eye and flinches.

"You need to get cleaned up first so you can see where the cuts are. See if you need stiches. Stay here." I whirl around and rush to grab the first aid kit from the bathroom.

When I return, Bast is slumped down low on one of the kitchen chairs. After I set the first aid kit on the table, I open it and fish around for what I need. Then I head over to the kitchen counter and wet a few paper towels before sitting in front of Bast.

"Tilt your face up."

He does as I ask but pulls away when I gently wipe his face.

"Stop moving," I grumble.

He stills, and once his face is clean, I can see that he has a cut near the corner of his eyebrow and one on his bottom lip. I grab the alcohol wipes from the first aid kit and bring one to his face to clean the cuts. Bast hisses.

"I don't think you'll need stitches. But you need to put some antibiotic ointment on them and keep them clean until they heal over." I wipe my hands with a clean alcohol wipe, then dot a bit of the ointment on my index finger before I coat his cuts.

It's clearly painful from the way Bast's jaw clenches, but he stays in place until I'm done.

"Now, tell me what happened."

He blows out a breath then winces.

"Bast"—I gently take his hand—"who did this to you?"

What kind of trouble has my brother gotten himself into?

"Bast…"

"Uma's goons."

My spine goes ramrod straight.

Uma Delvecchio is a high-level criminal who operates along the West Coast. As far as I know, she doesn't have any official association with the Mafia or any gangs, but she's the kind of person you want to stay away from. She's cold, heartless, and underhanded. She'll do whatever it takes to get what she wants and doesn't care who she has to hurt to do so.

As long as we've lived in this area, we've never had any association with her, so I cannot fathom why her guys would beat up my brother.

"Why would they do that? Please tell me you haven't gotten into bed with her?" My chest tightens when Bastion looks away. "Are you serious, Bast? Why the hell would you have anything to do with her?"

His jaw tightens, as does the fist he has on the table. He still won't look at me.

My stomach curdles. "What aren't you telling me?"

He stands from the chair and walks out of the kitchen without a word.

"Bastion! What the hell is going on?" The sinking feeling in my stomach sours as I follow him out into the living room. "Bastion!"

"It's not me. It's Dad. He made promises he couldn't follow through on."

The sinking feeling is a full-blown weight now, pulling me through the floor even though I'm still standing. "What? Why would he do that? When did he do that?"

Bastion whips around to look at me with accusing eyes. "A couple months after you left us in a lurch. And the why is obvious—money."

I fall onto the couch in a daze, trying to assemble the thoughts rolling through my head into something that makes sense. I'm so pissed at my dad for having anything to do with that woman after we've spent years trying to stay out of her way. "Why wouldn't he tell me?"

"For fuck's sake, Ari, first you want out, and now you're upset that Dad didn't give you the inside scoop on the scams he's running?"

I sink back into the seat. He's right. When I told them I wanted out, I made it clear that I wanted nothing more to do with their illegal activity. I didn't even want to know what they were up to.

With a sigh, I massage my temples. "Tell me what happened."

Bastion frowns and sits in the chair, gingerly moving to get himself comfortable with his sore ribs. "Dad went big this time. Bigger than he's ever gone. You don't need the details, but the gist is that he made promises to Uma he couldn't deliver on. Now Uma wants to be paid anyway. Plus interest."

"Did you have anything to do with it?" There's no hiding the accusation in my voice.

He scowls. "Of course not. If I'd known what he was up to before he went to see her, I would've stopped him. No payday is worth risking my life."

"So, how'd you find out?" I suck my bottom lip into my mouth, biting it.

"When I was out with Dad running a good Samaritan ruse, and her goons approached us. They made it clear that Uma was tired of waiting and that every day that passed, the interest accrued."

That explains my dad wanting to cash in on that billionaire I saved.

"You should have told me."

He scoffs. "What would you have done? Picked up an extra shift at the bar?" Bastion shakes his head.

That guilt that gnaws inside me because I left them digs deeper. "How much does he owe her?"

"It's a lot," he says. "Well over anything we've ever owed or swindled."

"How much, Bast?"

He sighs but tells me an amount that makes my breath come out in short spurts.

My dad will never be able to get that kind of money together. Not in this lifetime.

"What did her guys say to you tonight?" Tears overflow my eyes, blurring my vision as hopelessness spreads throughout my veins.

He presses his lips together and doesn't answer.

"Bastion, tell me."

"They said he has three months to pay up. Otherwise, they'll pay another visit to me." He swallows hard. "And you."

The fine hairs on the back of my neck prickle.

I cannot believe my father got us into this mess. But should I really be surprised? He's been pushing the limits for years. Getting into more and more unsavory things. Never satisfied. Always looking for the big payoff. The one that will leave him set for life. Which is why I finally opted out of the family business.

Running scams at the local flea market or on other criminals was one thing. Taking elderly people's life savings is quite another. I just couldn't do it anymore, even if it ostracized me from the only family I have.

The two of us sit in silence for a couple of minutes. I'm trying to take in the information, come up with some type of feasible plan even though it doesn't feel as though there is one. Bastion is probably just thinking about how fucked we are since this isn't news to him.

"We could run," I say.

He looks at the ceiling. "Might buy us some time, but you know she'll find us."

"Yeah…" The last thing I want—besides being tortured and murdered because of my dad's poor decision-making—is to be looking over my shoulder for the rest of my life. Always wondering if today is the day my past catches up with me.

"Face it, we're fucked, Ari."

I shake my head. "No. There has to be something we can do." My hand goes up to the gold locket that hangs around my neck, and I slide the smooth metal between my thumb and index finger.

"What are you going to do—ask Uma?" Bastion laughs because it's a completely absurd idea but…

"That's exactly what I'm going to do."

CHAPTER

FIVE

ARIANA

"You can't just walk in there uninvited, Ari."

The only reason Bastion is in the driver's seat beside me is so I know he won't go tattle to our dad. But I'm sick of listening to him, and I'm this close to sending him back home.

"Watch me. She wants her money, or she wouldn't have made an example of you last night. It's not going to do her any good to kill me on sight."

I sound more confident than I feel. There's no way for me to know how Uma will react. I've never actually met the woman, though I've seen her at a distance when some of her goons came into the bar where I work and dragged someone off a bar stool in front of me. I never saw him again, something I push out of my mind the minute it flickers.

I had to call in sick at the law firm today to be here, and I plan to make it count even if my hand shakes when I reach the car door handle.

Bastion grips my arm before I can exit the car. "I should come with you."

I give him a small smile and shake my head. "No, I'll take this one."

He smiles, and my heart warms because I haven't seen him look at me like that since before I told him and Dad I wanted out. "It's good to have you back on the team."

I barely suppress an eyeroll and don't mention that once this situation is fixed—*if* it can be fixed—I'm back on the bench.

As I get out of the car, my breath catches from the sensation of being watched. I have no doubt that Uma is already well aware of my visit. The cameras aren't in obscure places, hidden from view. They're in spots designed to make it abundantly clear we're not alone.

I have no idea where her home is, but everyone around here knows where she runs her business. At least anyone with any kind of tie to the criminal world. So I approach the rundown warehouse she does business out of. When I reach the metal door on the side of the building, I knock, then step back, swallowing past the dryness in my throat.

The door creaks open, and a big burly guy with a shaved head and a scar down his face stands on the other side. He doesn't say anything, just grunts and lifts his chin at me. I take it to mean he wants me to say who I am.

"I'm here to see Uma." Though I do my best to project confidence, I'm not sure I succeed. I'm way out of my element but showing any kind of weakness to her would be a mistake. So I plan to walk in here with big dick energy I don't actually feel and hope it gets me somewhere.

"She's not expecting anyone." He starts to shut the door, but I put my hand on it.

"I need to see her. It's important."

He gives me the once-over before jerking his head to the side. A gesture I take to mean come in. Whether it does or doesn't, I step inside, and I'm no more than two steps from him when he brings me to a stop with a meaty hand on my elbow.

"You don't go in until I pat you down."

I glance down at my skintight short-sleeve shirt and leggings. Where the hell would I hide a weapon? But it's probably not about making sure his boss is safe and more about the intimidation factor, so I spread my legs and hold my arms out from my sides. "Have at it."

He starts at my ankles and works his way up my legs, making sure to pay extra attention to my ass and my breasts, but I don't say anything. I merely suck in a breath, knowing full well this is all part of his plan to scare me.

When he's finished, he grunts and walks forward. I assume he wants me to follow.

He leads me through the warehouse, but there's not much to see. There're a couple shipping containers and some other boxes, but nothing worth noting. When we arrive at an office in the back corner, he raps on the door, and a muffled, "Come in," sounds from behind the door.

He swings it open, and I get my first close-up look at Uma Delvecchio. Her black hair hangs past her shoulders, and her dark eyes take me in with a hint of amusement. She props her legs up on the desk in front of her, crossing her ankles.

Unlike the rest of the place, her office has been decorated to the nines with a polished marble floor and sleek black furniture. It feels more fitting for the woman who's studying me intently, wearing designer everything, than the rest of the warehouse.

"Ariana, to what do I owe the pleasure?" She arches a perfectly shaped eyebrow.

I step past the beast of a man, not sparing him a glance. "You know exactly why I'm here. Let's not play games." I sit in the chair across from her desk without waiting for the invitation.

Her eyes spark, and one corner of her mouth lifts. Her expression reminds me of a cat who's found a new and entertaining mouse to play with.

"Nothing comes to mind." She grins, looks at the guy still standing at the door, and nods.

He doesn't say anything, and I hear the door close behind me.

Uma settles her eyes back on me. She's intimidating. I can feel her sizing me up, looking for cracks in my armor.

I decide to get right down to the problem. No sense beating around the bush. "I want to know what I can do to get you to back off."

"Well, that's simple." She holds her hand out in front of her, studying her cherry red nails. "Pay me my money."

I hold her gaze. "You know that's not possible."

"Then I guess your dad shouldn't make promises he can't keep." She arches an eyebrow.

She's not wrong, and we both know it.

"Give us some more time to come up with the money." I hate the pleading note to my voice.

She appraises me, and her legs drop from the desk to the floor as she straightens in her seat. "Us? Rumor has it you left the family business."

I don't know how she knows that—whether my brother or dad alluded to it—but it doesn't matter. She probably knows everything about us. You don't get to where she is without properly sizing up your competition.

"I find myself back in. At least until this matter is resolved."

She nods knowingly, as though there's something I'm not saying but don't need to because she knows me so well. Even though this is our first face-to-face.

"Why not leave your father to face the consequences of his own actions?"

"He's my father," I say. *Plus, you've made it clear that Bastion and I will be collateral damage.* But I don't add that.

"Loyalty. I like that. I could use that..." She lets the unspoken invitation hang between us.

I shake my head and fist my hands. "Not interested."

"Are you sure?" She gives me the once-over. "I could use someone like you. Young, beautiful, beguiling. Men never give us women the wide berth we deserve, do they? They constantly underestimate us. How do you think I got where I am?"

"The way I hear it, you betrayed your mentor, killed him, and then filled the void." The words fly out of my mouth before I can stop them. I stiffen in my seat, waiting for her reaction. For all I know, she has a gun under that desk, and for insulting her, she'll put a bullet in my head.

To my relief, she laughs. "Oh, I definitely like you. Maybe I should wipe your dad's slate clean in exchange for having you come work for me."

My stomach lurches. "Not happening. Now will you give us more time to come up with the money or not?"

She stands from her chair and places her palms on the desk, leaning closer to me. The façade of an amused villain is gone. Now she looks like a sociopath. There's zero emotion in her eyes. "Not a chance. A deal is a deal, and a debt is a debt. You have three months to get me my money or face the consequences."

My jaw hardens, and I force myself to hold in the panic wrapping around my throat like barbed wire. I stand from the chair. "Fine. You'll have your money."

Though I have no idea how.

"How are you going to come up with that kind of money?" Her head tilts, and the movement looks so animalistic that I suppress a shiver.

"That's not for you to worry about."

She grins and her eyes dart to the necklace around my neck—the one thing my mother left me before she took off. My hand flies up to cover it.

"That looks like it might be worth something. Why not hand it over? I'll put it toward what your father owes me."

I shake my head. "No way."

Her grin intensifies, and I realize that I've made the mistake of letting her know that this necklace means something to me. That it's not some costume piece, but it holds sentimental meaning. Sometimes I question why, given that I barely even remember my mother.

Uma holds her hand out between us. "Hand it over."

My fist tightens around the gold locket. "I said I'll get you your money. We still have three months."

"Consider it collateral. If you give me the money you owe me, you get it back."

We stare at each other for at least a minute, and it's clear she won't back down. Anger boils my blood because she's only doing this to make me suffer, to see me squirm. Not because she really wants the necklace.

Jaw tight, I unclasp the necklace and hand it over. My stomach sinks when it drops into her waiting palm. I turn and walk to the door.

When my hand is on the handle, she says, "And don't even think of trying to bolt. I'll find you."

Without responding, I whip open the door and walk with purpose through the warehouse. I just want to get the hell out of this place before the walls close in on me.

No one confronts me as I make my way to the door I came in through and head back outside. My brother's eyes widen when he sees me and relief pours over his features, his hands tight around the steering wheel.

I whip open the passenger door, get in, and slam it closed. "Go."

He doesn't say anything to me. Just flicks his gaze in my direction every so often until he finally pulls the car into the parking lot of a fast-food place. "What happened?"

"We're fucked, that's what happened. Dad screwed us." I squeeze my eyes shut, finally calming my breathing and heart rate.

"She won't give us more time to come up with the money?"

His use of the word us reminds me of what Uma said, and my anger flares at my dad for dragging me back into the life I'm trying so hard to leave.

"No. She made it clear there will be no deals." I blow out a breath. "What are we going to do?"

I turn my head to look at Bastion and nearly wince when I take in the swelling and bruises on his face. I can't bear for him to go through another beating or worse, torture.

Plus, I'm lucky I haven't received the same treatment yet.

He stares at the roof of the car. "No idea."

I think back to what my dad said about the billionaire I rescued. Maybe I could try to get some money out of him for saving his life. But the problem remains that there's no way to prove it was me. I'm sure I'd be one of a bunch of gold-diggers trying to cash in.

My hand goes to the locket, to finger it while I think, but my chest is bare, a swift reminder that Uma has it. "I'll figure something out. In the meantime, you make sure Dad doesn't get himself into any more trouble."

"Yeah, okay." He's quiet before he rolls the back of his head on the headrest and turns to me. "Thanks for not leaving me to deal with this on my own."

I squeeze his hand. Bastion can drive me crazy most of the time, but I've always had a soft spot for him. He didn't stand a chance after the situation he left so young, ending up on the streets, then having my dad influence his path.

"That's what family does."

He and my dad may not be perfect, but they stuck around. And that counts for something.

CHAPTER

SIX

ARIANA

I'm on my laptop, trying to find out everything I can about Obsidian Voss, billionaire. So far, there isn't much. It appears the Voss brothers are intensely private, and most of what I can dig up is business related.

Obsidian, or Sid as he is mostly referred to, is thirty-four years old. He's a lawyer and in charge of the legal department at Voss Enterprises, overseeing their vast number of holdings.

Nothing states he's married. The women he's photographed with are young, beautiful, and come from the same world he does.

I'm keenly aware of how hot the man is. Typically, I'm not into older guys—god knows I've had enough of them hit on me at the bar—but something about this man draws me in. Makes my gaze linger on his perfect profile and his eyes so dark they almost look black. The wolf tattoo on his neck feels like a warning against the handsome, put-together man in a three-piece suit. As though something is lurking beneath the surface. A predator.

When I rescued him, it was apparent he was attractive and fit, muscular, but I was too busy saving his life to really look at him. In one picture my eyes haven't been able to stray from for the past five minutes, he's looking right into the camera with an intensity in his stare I've never seen. It's almost as though he can see into me, down into my soul, even through the photo.

A shiver works its way up my spine.

It's been a couple days since my meeting with Uma, and I'm still not sure what to do. No amount of googling has produced any evidence that Sid is looking to find the person who saved him. Maybe my instincts were right, and he was trying to end his life.

If I attempt to contact him, I'll come off like a scammer trying to fleece him. I'm thinking it's a complete loss until I see my in.

"What the hell were you thinking going to see Uma?"

My dad's voice startles me, and I slam my laptop closed. "Jesus, you scared me."

"*I* scared you? She should scare you. You should never have gone there!"

My dad is an easy-going guy and hardly ever gets mad. When I brought home a D in math my sophomore year of high school because I was more into partying and following Tommy Benson around than I was in my classes, he didn't bat an eye. Then again, he never was a believer in traditional education. The only time he ever really gets pissed at Bastion or me is when we mess up a scam. Then he acts as if it's the end of the world, ranting and raving.

I look at him over my shoulder. "What did you expect me to do? Have you seen Bastion?" It's his fault Bast looks like a piñata after a six-year-old's birthday party.

"You're the one who wanted out, Ariana."

I lurch up from the chair to face him, hands fisted at my sides. "Yeah, but now you've forced me back in. I'm not just going to let her kill you. What the hell were you thinking getting involved with her in the first place?"

He lifts his chin, looking down his nose at me. "I was thinking about one last big payday, and I could get out of this shit. That maybe you'd be proud of me if I did. That we'd all be free from this life."

My shoulders sag. It's possible he believes what he's saying, but I know it for what it is—a lie. Whether to himself or to me to make me feel more guilty than I already do, I don't know. My entire life, my dad has been chasing the next big payday, and he's never found it.

"You should have never gotten into bed with her. You know it. Look at the position we're all in now."

"You just worry about yourself, Ari, like you have been doing. Bast and I have been managing just fine on our own these past six months."

My lips press into a thin line. "I'd beg to differ."

He scowls and stomps over to the fridge, grabbing a beer. At least it's nine o'clock at night and not nine in the morning.

He twists the beer cap off and tosses it in the sink. "It's not your problem to worry about."

Rolling my eyes, I walk over and pluck the cap from the stainless steel and open the cupboard door under the sink, tossing it in the garbage can.

"You've made it my problem. Don't worry, I'll fix it." I walk back over to the kitchen table and pick up my laptop, then head to my bedroom.

"How're you gonna come up with that money?" my dad says.

"I'm going to go get myself a job with a billionaire," I mumble.

It was no easy feat, but I did it.

After an interview with HR, a skills test, and an interview with one very intense Asher Voss, CEO of Voss Enterprises, I am now the assistant of Obsidian Voss. Why he didn't interview me himself since I'll be assisting him, I have no idea.

The only thing I was really nervous about was the background check. I don't know why. Neither my dad, nor my brother or I have a record. We've never been caught or charged for any of the scams we ran—it was one of the tenets of our upbringing. Never attract the attention of the authorities. If we ever thought we may have, we'd haul ass out of town and set up shop somewhere else under a different name.

When I saw the job opening on the Voss Enterprises website and how well my qualifications lined up with what they were looking for, I knew this was my in. The best part is that as a part of the job, I'll be living at the Voss family home, which undoubtedly means access to all kinds of expensive things I can steal and sell. And not for a little money. A *lot* of money. Billionaires don't have two-dollar tchotchkes adorning their mansions.

I don't feel good about going back to the life of a thief, but it's necessary to save my family and myself. Besides, billionaires? They probably won't even notice anything is missing.

I'm booked in a first-class seat, and a driver picks me up from the airport to drive me to the Voss family estate. My stomach feels like a witch's cauldron, bubbling with nerves the longer I'm snug in the leather seat of the fancy car.

The driver doesn't speak, so I don't say anything to him. I sit silently in the back seat and watch the city streets turn into country roads until we stop in front of a large set of iron gates.

This must be it. My hand falls to my stomach.

The driver punches in a code, and the gates slowly ease open. We drive down a winding road with large, old trees on either side. Eventually, the trees stop, and I get my first glimpse of my new home.

Holy shit.

The place is enormous. Bigger than enormous. Unfathomably big. I didn't even know houses like this existed outside of movies.

Even more than that, this place looks as if it's been pulled out of a Dracula novel or something. There are a couple of stone gargoyles on the top of the building. The dark stone sucks in the sunlight, and the large towers at each end of the massive building give it an old-world castle feel.

The driver stops in front of the enormous front door with stained glass above it and gets out of the car. I use the moment alone to take a deep breath and slowly blow it out.

Before I'm prepared, he opens the car door and helps me out. I'm not used to the humidity in the south, and I've been covered in a thin layer of perspiration since landing. All my clothes cling to my body like a second skin.

"Your bags will be brought to your room. I believe Marcel, the house manager, is waiting for you inside. He'll direct you where to go," he says.

I give him a small smile and nod my thanks before approaching the door and knocking. It opens almost immediately to a smiling man I assume is Marcel.

"Good day, Miss Clarke. Welcome to Midnight Manor."

I had no idea that's what this place was called, but from what I've seen thus far, the description fits. I step inside. "Thank you."

The inside is adorned much the way I expected. Which means richly with a lot of antique pieces. Even though it's daytime, sconces flicker on the walls because the light from outside doesn't penetrate the arched windows. At least from what I can see. The house is dim, and you'd never think the summer sun is shining outside.

"Mr. Voss is expecting you. I'm to take you to his office. Follow me please."

"Sure." I walk alongside him.

It doesn't take long before I'm turned around and unsure how to get back to where we started. It goes against all my instincts. My dad always told us to make sure we cataloged all the exits of anywhere we went. You never know when you might need to make a quick escape.

"Um... which Mr. Voss are we going to meet?"

Marcel looks at me. "Sorry. Asher Voss. I believe he wants to meet with you before Obsidian joins you."

I nod, feeling a little better that my first meeting will be with a man with whom I've already interacted. Even if he is extremely intense and not that friendly.

We continue down a wide hallway with a high arched ceiling and stained-glass windows on one side.

"This place is a maze. How do you remember where to go?" I ask.

Marcel chuckles. "You'll get used to it, I assure you."

I'm not sure I believe him, but I smile at him anyway.

We stop in front of a large wooden door, and he knocks.

"Come in," I hear from the other side.

Marcel opens the door and motions for me to enter. "Miss Clarke is here, sir."

Asher Voss glances at me, then looks at my chaperone.

"Thanks, Marcel. Can you please ask Sid to join us in five minutes?"

Marcel nods and turns without saying anything.

"Miss Clarke, have a seat." Asher motions in front of me.

I enter the room and notice another person in here with us. A beautiful brunette walks toward Asher's desk from the far corner. Her smile puts me at ease, at least as much as I can be in this moment.

I've always struggled with the beginning stages of a ruse. My dad used to say he could see it on me and nagged me about fixing the fact I struggle to lie.

When she gets close, she holds out her hand. "I'm Anabelle. It's good to meet you."

I shake her hand. "Ariana Clarke."

"Anabelle is my wife," Asher says, and the pride in his voice at his proclamation makes me like Asher Voss.

"Oh. You make a very nice couple," I say to them, needing to butter up everyone I'm interacting with so they don't see through me.

Anabelle playfully rolls her eyes as though she finds her husband amusing and leans her hip against the side of Asher's desk as I sit.

Asher says, "I wanted to touch base with you before you go off with Obsidian to let you know what you're walking into."

I fight to keep the smile on my face, but I'm not sure I'm successful.

"He's not exactly thrilled that I've hired you," Asher says.

My stomach tightens, and my breakfast threatens to rush back up. "He's not?" I assumed when the job was posted it was because Obsidian wanted an assistant.

Anabelle gives me a sympathetic look while Asher shakes his head, mouth turned down in a frown. "No. But he needs an assistant to relieve some of the pressure he's under, take some things off his plate."

I nod. "Okay, I appreciate the heads-up." Hopefully, once Obsidian realizes what an asset I can be to him, he'll change his attitude.

"If I know my brother, he's going to attempt to get you to quit. He'll be a dick and make things difficult for you."

Wonderful. I'm not sure what to say to that, so I say nothing.

"If it becomes too much for you, come see me, and I'll deal with him."

I nod, knowing I'll handle whatever Obsidian Voss dishes out because I need to remain in this house until I can fence enough stuff to pay back my father's debt.

"Good. Hopefully what we're paying you will help take some of the sting off his attitude," Asher says.

Now it makes sense why this job pays what it does. It's about three times what anywhere else would pay, and I'd assumed it was because Obsidian works day and night. But it seems like it's danger pay because he plans to be an asshole. Even with the good money I'm making, it would be decades before I could pay Uma off.

Doesn't matter. I'll take whatever he's going to dish out and smile while I'm doing it. My family's lives—hell, my life—depend on it.

"I'm sure it won't be a problem." I smile at them both, but the wan smile on Anabelle's face gives me pause.

Before Asher can respond, there's a knock on the door. I turn to look over my shoulder and spot Obsidian Voss stalking into the room like a predator on the hunt, and I steel myself for his wrath.

CHAPTER
SEVEN

I prowl into Asher's office, pissed off and not bothering to cover it up with a polished veneer. No sense pretending this will be anything other than what it will be—painful. Painful for her and painful for me. Let whoever this woman Asher hired to be my sidekick get what so few people do—a glimpse behind my façade.

Asher and Anabelle both look away from the woman in front of them as I enter.

"Sid, thanks for joining us," Asher says, as though he's given me a choice.

I don't answer, sliding my hands into my pockets when I reach the opposite side of his desk.

If I'd pressed my brothers on not hiring an assistant, they'd only try to use it as leverage to insist that something is going on with me and then we'd have to talk about our fucking feelings. Talk about what happened so long ago and whether it had anything to do with what happened to me in the ocean.

Yeah, no thanks. I'd rather deal with the assistant and just get rid of her of her own free will. It's the path of least resistance at this point.

"This is your new assistant, Ariana Clarke." Asher motions across the desk.

For the first time, I give her my attention. It feels like a blow to the stomach, as if the wind's been knocked out of me.

She's gorgeous. Stunning.

I've seen a lot of beautiful women in my time. Fucked a lot of them, too. But this woman... something about her... I don't know. It's almost as though she's vaguely familiar, but it's more than that.

Every one of her features feels tailor-made to draw me in. From her long, brilliant red hair cascading in waves to the wash of innocent freckles over her cheeks and her slightly upturned nose. Those pink, puffy lips of hers are slightly parted, and her big blue eyes stare up at me, assessing. It all comes together in a way that makes her perfect.

"It's nice to meet you, sir. I look forward to working together," she says, and fuck me, her voice is so feminine and innocent-sounding that my dick twitches under my tailored suit pants.

"Wish I could say the same."

I'm impressed when she doesn't blink at my comment. Asher must have given her the heads-up that I'd be a prick. I suppose that means I'll have to double my efforts.

"Marcel is going to make sure that all of Miss Clarke's things are brought to her room. Perhaps you could show her there, and I figured you'd want to show her where she'll be working. Perhaps give her a tour of the rest of the manor and grounds," Asher says.

I shift my attention to him. "I'm not a tour guide."

His jaw tics and his expression hardens. "True. But I'm sure you can handle it." He gives me a look that I read as, "stop screwing around," but I turn back to Ariana.

"Let's go." I don't wait to see if she follows.

When I reach the hallway, her heels echo on the marble floor just behind me. Without a word, I lead her out of the west wing, Asher's private area, through the common part of the estate, and over to the east wing where I reside. I swear I hear her gasp when we walk through the long hallway of stained glass from the common area into my wing, especially as we walk past the large wolf window. I feel the weight of her gaze on the wolf tattoo on my neck as if she's piecing something together.

The first place I take her is my office, where someone has set up a desk for her. Swinging open the double doors, I motion for her to go in ahead of me. To my surprise, there's no fear or trepidation in her eyes. She steps into the wood-paneled room, and the scent of coconuts and something floral washes past me, reminding me of a tropical beach.

My gaze dips down her body, and I take in the way her dress pants curve over her ass. I'm forced to stifle a groan because this woman has an ass made to be bare and on display.

"How old are you?" I ask, walking past her then turning to face her.

"Twenty-four." She lifts her chin a bit as though daring me to say she's too young to do the job or something.

So young. So innocent.

"Think you can handle me?" I arch an eyebrow and slide my hands in my pockets. I expect her to look uncomfortable at the double entendre, but she merely smirks.

"I'm sure I can."

"What makes you so sure of that?" I step closer to her.

Again with the smirk. "I've dealt with bigger, badder people than you, Mr. Voss."

A chuckle leaves my lips of its own accord. "I'm not your typical lawyer in a three-piece suit, Miss Clarke."

She gives me a patronizing smile. "I wasn't talking about lawyers in suits."

Stepping around me, she takes in the room with its built-in bookcases and wood paneling, sitting area set off to the side, and my desk, kitty-corner to her own.

This woman is intriguing, I'll give her that. But she still needs to go.

I show her around the office and tell her a little bit about how a typical day goes, then I give her the ground rules. "You're to be on time to work every day, and I expect you to be by my side and anticipate my every need throughout the workday. If I travel, you'll be expected to travel with me. Your work must be done correctly. There's no room for mistakes. We're not talking about a little mom-and-pop shop here. Voss Enterprises deals with billions of dollars in assets, hundreds of companies, and tens of thousands of employees. What we do affects each of those things, so like I said—zero room for error. Once our workday is done, I don't want to see you again until the next day. And the most important thing to remember is that you work for me, *not* my brothers."

She nods. "Got it. What time do you want me here tomorrow morning?"

"Six sharp. My day starts early."

She merely nods, and inwardly I chuckle because she'll be sitting here for a long while before I show up.

"I'll show you to your room now." I walk past her without waiting for her and continue down the hallway.

I've put her on the same side of the hallway as me, but on the very far end.

"This will be your room. You should have everything you need, but if you find you don't, you can use the bedside phone and track down Marcel. He can arrange to get you whatever you need. The en suite is here." I step over to the open door and motion inside.

Ariana steps into the bathroom door frame and looks inside, not saying a tword. Her closeness seems to register with my body, and my heart picks up speed.

Swallowing, I turn away from her and walk into the large closet. When I step inside, I see that Marcel has already had her things delivered to her room and unpacked. Clothes hang in the closet, and shoes have been placed on the shoe rack.

"This is your closet. I'm not sure what kind of clothing you brought, but I expect professional dress at all times when you're working. Especially when we travel. You're representing Voss Enterprises and therefore me, so you should be impeccably dressed."

Her gaze runs over my custom suit, one of the plethora I have direct from Savile Row in London.

In turn, my gaze coasts over her dress pants and flowing white tank made from cheap material. "If you can't afford the proper attire, let me know, and I'll make arrangements."

Her cheeks pinken a bit at my not-so-subtle dig. "I will, thank you."

Liking the fact that I've finally managed to unnerve her somewhat, I decide to push it to the next level and step over to the row of drawers in the center island of the closet, guessing what I'll find there. I slide one open and see that I'm right. Marcel has placed all her underwear in the top drawer. Various colors of lace panties and thongs are stacked, and I have to bite back a groan when my mind instantly goes to what they would look like on Ariana's body.

I pull out one and make a show of studying it, then lift it between us. "Seems Marcel did an excellent job of unpacking all your things." My voice is low.

Ariana's face grows redder, but she lifts her chin in defiance. "I'll be sure to thank him."

Oh, she'll be a fun one to break.

I drop the underwear from the end of my finger, and it falls back into the drawer. "I'll leave you to get settled."

"What about the tour of the manor and the grounds?" she asks.

I'd forgotten about that. More than anything, I'm surprised she'd want to prolong her time with me. "Ask Marcel to have someone else do it. I have things to do."

I stalk out of the closet, out of the room, and out of the east wing entirely. Something about that woman gets under my skin, and I need whatever distance I can put between us now because beginning tomorrow, she'll be by my side nearly constantly.

EIGHT

ARIANA

At two minutes to six, I arrive in Obsidian's office, and I'm not at all surprised to find that I'm alone. When he told me what time to be here, I fully suspected he might be setting me up to run me ragged every day. But what he doesn't know is that I'm determined to stay in his house for as long as possible. At least long enough to steal enough things to pay off my father's debt to Uma.

I've thought about what might happen if I'm caught and decided I don't care. What will these brothers do? Fire me? A much better option than what Uma will do. I just have to make sure if I get caught, it's not until *after* I've paid off the debt. If I have to go to jail in order to ensure that my dad, my brother, and I can keep breathing, it will suck, but it's worth it.

What Obsidian didn't realize was that leaving me alone gives me time to snoop. I take the opportunity to study everything in the office. It would be stupid to steal something from this room, though. Given all the time Obsidian probably spends here, he'd be more likely to notice. So far. I'm surprised I haven't seen any cameras.

But after a few minutes of studying, it's apparent that my instinct to come here was right—the manor is filled with expensive items. I'll have to go exploring whenever I'm done with work for the day.

I never did get a tour yesterday. My mind was preoccupied with whether Obsidian would recognize me from the beach. A part of me was disappointed he didn't. It would have made all of this easier if I'd been able to say, "Yes, it was me who saved you, can I have a few million as a reward?"

Not wanting to venture out into the intimidating manor by myself last night, I remained in my room and watched a few shows on my laptop, then read. Thankfully, Marcel showed up and informed me that my meals would be delivered to my room. I have no idea whether everyone who resides here eats in their room, but I was happy to eat in solace.

A tour would have been useful, but I wanted the excuse to say I'm trying to figure out how to navigate the place if anyone found me skulking around while I was looking for things to steal.

In my short time in Obsidian's presence yesterday, he made it clear that Asher was correct, he's definitely going to do his best to make me quit. It was also obvious that I am going to have to watch myself around Obsidian. Intelligence and challenge gleam behind his dark eyes, and if I'm not careful, he'll figure out there's more to me than just a young woman who's eager to do a good job for the billion-aire brothers who hired her.

Then you add on his incredibly good looks, and it's just another layer that makes him so dangerous. His suit fit him perfectly, showcasing his fit body. The way his dark wavy hair hung off to one side over the short hair on the side of his head made him look as though he was ready to step onto a runway in Milan. His entire presence is intense and dominating, as though he's assessing everything around him at all times.

I give my head a shake. Enough of thinking about how my new boss is hot as hell. I need to prove to him that I belong here, that I can be a help to him. Doing so will only make things easier for me while I'm here.

So I get to work. I haven't really been told what my daily tasks involve, but I open the laptop on my desk and use the password I set up with Voss Enterprises to log in, finding Obsidian's email as well as one for me.

Obviously part of my job will be sorting through his emails, so I get to work. Once I've flagged everything that looks like something he should deal with directly, I print them and put them in descending order of urgency and set them on his desk. It's obvious that he prefers hard copies of the things he's working on. Then I forward any emails I can deal with to my email address, write down a list of ques-tions I have about them, and forward them to my contact at Voss Enterprises.

Brynne is Obsidian's main go-to at the head office. I have no idea how she feels about me being hired to assist him day-to-day in his home office, but she's the contact HR gave me.

I'm just finishing when Obsidian decides to grace me with his presence.

"Good morning," I say in a cheery voice, giving him no insight into whether or not I'm agitated that he's showing up so late after instructing me to be here at six.

Today he's wearing a black three-piece suit with a cream shirt and a red tie. I spot the tattoo on his neck as he walks past, and I suppress the urge to lick my lips when my mind conjures up an image of me running my tongue over it.

Jesus, get a grip, Ari.

"Have you been waiting long?" He takes a seat at his desk with a small grin.

What an ass.

I stand and walk toward him. "No problem at all. It gave me some time to get the lay of the land. I've gone through your email and printed off what you need to respond to yourself, then sent the rest to my email. I'll take care of those for you, and I can cc you on them if you like." I sit in the chair across from his desk.

He actually looks surprised, but he nods in agreement, then his face goes blank.

"Wonderful. Would you like to dictate to me your responses to those emails on your desk"—I nod toward the pile—"or do you prefer to respond to them yourself?"

"Quite the waste of resources to print all of these off when they're readily available on the computer, don't you think?" There's disdain in his features as he arches a dark eyebrow.

I smile sweetly. "I assumed you weren't concerned with that when I saw the state of your desk." I motion to the stacks of papers that very clearly could have been read on the computer.

He grumbles something under his breath.

"What was that?" I ask.

"I said grab your computer, and I'll dictate my responses to you." He picks up the first piece of paper to read.

I get up from the chair and walk back over to my desk, positive I feel his gaze on me the entire way. But when I grab the laptop and turn back around, he's looking at the paper in his hand. Maybe it was wishful thinking on my part, which is beyond ridiculous. I'm here to accomplish one thing, and it does not involve crushing on a hot older man who's so far out of my reach that it isn't funny.

I sit and set the laptop on his desk. "Which one would you like to respond to first?"

BY SIX THAT NIGHT, I'm dying to get out of these heels, and my stomach is growling. I've been working for twelve hours, and it's not that I'm not accustomed to it—I've worked two jobs for a while now—but being in Obsidian's presence all day and pretending not to be affected is sucking up my energy. Every time his ebony eyes land on me, it feels like a whisper of a touch, and I'm dying to know what he's thinking. Every time he makes some snide comment or acts like a dick, the effort it takes not to come back at him is immense. I need a break—from him, not necessarily the work.

But I'll be damned if I ask him if I can leave first. No, he'll have to tell me we're done for the day. I'll play this all day.

"Damn it." His voice travels across the room.

I glance over to see him hitting a button on his keyboard over and over, frustration etched along his mouth. "Can I help you with something?"

He flicks his gaze in my direction. "Not unless you're an IT expert," he practically growls.

I walk over to his desk and stand beside him. This is the closest I've been to him today, and the scent of his expensive cologne—leather and brandy—is almost edible.

"What seems to be the problem?"

He gestures to the computer with the flick of his wrist. "You tell me."

I bend toward his screen, reaching for his keyboard. The spinning beach ball that only means trouble rolls in a circle in the middle of his screen. I hit a few keys, and nothing happens.

"It's fucked."

I turn to look at him and realize how close we are. His face can't be more than six inches from mine. Our gazes lock and hold before I blink and spin back to the computer, swallowing hard.

"Let me try something. Were you working on something that needs to be saved?"

"No." The one word comes out gravelly compared to his normal voice. Is it possible he's as affected as I am by our close proximity?

I close out of what programs I can and hit a few more keys, waiting patiently until the window comes up asking whether I want to force a shutdown. Every one of my breaths is shallower than the last, and I'm hyper aware that all he has to do is flick his gaze to his left, and he'll be staring at my ass.

I force the shutdown and stay in place to see if it worked. When a large hand cups my left hip, I still before I find Obsidian's hand there, expensive watch gleaming under the lights. The heat from his hand seeps through the fabric of my skirt, and I wouldn't be surprised if he just branded me.

The computer sounds, and I turn to see the start-up screen waiting for a sign-in. "That should do it." I straighten, and his hand falls.

He clears his throat as I step away. "Great, that should be it for today. You don't need to come in until seven tomorrow morning."

I turn to face him, but he's not looking at me. His fingers are poised on the keyboard, and he's signing back into his computer, paying me no mind.

"See you then." I scurry back to my desk to sign out of my computer before bolting from the room.

As soon as I reach my bedroom, I swing the door closed and collapse back against it.

What was that? Is he trying to freak me out and make me uncomfortable so I'll quit? Or is he attracted to me too?

What does it even matter if he is? Getting involved with him will only make things more complicated for me. I'm here to steal from this man, not fall for him.

Under no circumstances can I get involved with Obsidian Voss.

He's the kind of man who would chew me up and spit me out. I do not need more problems in my life, only solutions. So I can look, but I cannot touch. No matter what.

CHAPTER

NINE

ARIANA

The next morning, Obsidian acts as though nothing happened and is his usual non-charming self. As the day passes, I realize what a juxtaposition his attitude toward me is compared to the way he interacts with everyone else.

To me, he's short and snippy, outright rude, and somewhat condescending. On the phone, he's charming and irreverent, sounding like a different man completely.

By the end of the week, I'm still trying to figure out which version of him is the real one.

But I put all that aside because it's Saturday, and tonight, I have to meet my brother at the local dive bar to pass off something for him to sell. I can't chance selling anything myself. Besides, it's not like a local pawn shop is going to give me a decent price. This way my brother can reach out to the many contacts we've made over the years and get a better price.

The only problem is that I haven't snagged anything. At first, I told myself I didn't want to do it too early because that would mean I had to hide it somewhere in my room and the longer it was missing, the better chance they'd suspect me and find wherever I stashed it.

But the truth is that I've seen a few items I can take, had the opportunity to do so, and I've chickened out. The Vosses may be able to afford to replace the items and may not even notice anything is gone, given how much they have, but it's the principle of it all. There's a reason I left the family business. My conscience is fighting me.

So the first time I went for the Fabergé egg, my hand just couldn't wrap around it.

But I'm out of time. I'm about to leave to head to the bar and meet my brother, so I have no choice.

I find my way to the room in question, which is in the common area of the manor, and stop when I get inside, listening for anyone. The room is dim, as they all are—especially once the sun starts setting—and long shadows cast upon the wall courtesy of the flickering sconces on the walls. I make my way toward the table where the egg sits. I purposely wore my larger purse tonight so that I would have room for it without attracting notice.

Knowing that hesitation is what gets you caught, I walk past the table, swipe it, and slide it into my bag. My heart hammers, and I feel as though I'm lugging around a fifty-pound weight in my bag.

Marcel's by the front door, and I panic a bit, my throat closing.

"Hello, Miss Clarke. I just wanted to see you off and to give you this." He holds out a black business card. On it is a phone number printed in white. "When you're ready to return to the manor, just text this number, and the driver will come and get you."

My shoulders relax. "Thank you so much, I appreciate it." I'd contacted Marcel earlier today to see if I could arrange a ride down the hill into the town of Magnolia Bend.

"My pleasure. Have a good evening." He nods and walks away.

I sigh, walking out the door, and slip in the back seat of the car. The driver doesn't say a word to me as he drives toward the gates.

It takes no time before we're in front of Black Magic Bar.

"Thank you for the ride," I say and get out of the car.

When I step inside the bar, I look around. It's definitely a dive bar, yet...different. I suppose it's on theme with the name because there are nods to magic throughout the place. But all of that falls to the wayside when I spot Bastion sitting at one of the tables with a hand raised and a smile on his face.

I rush over, only now realizing how much I've missed him. He might drive me a little crazy, but living at Midnight Manor and pretending to be there for reasons I'm not has left me feeling lonely.

He stands as I get closer to the table. "Hey, stranger. How are you?" I give him a big hug and he seems taken aback. "Hey, everything all right?"

"Yeah, just a little homesick."

He frowns as we both sit at the table. "You sure you can handle this? It's been less than a week."

I hook my purse on the back of my chair, the contents within feeling like a homing beacon for everyone in this bar. "Of course I can. I have no choice. How's Dad? Staying out of trouble?"

He sighs. "Mostly."

My eyes narrow. "What's that mean? You're supposed to be keeping an eye on him."

Bastion rolls his eyes. "You know what he's like. He can't help himself."

"What kind of scam is he running now?" I lean back in my seat with my arms crossed, unimpressed.

He waves off my concern. "Don't worry about it. I'll keep him in check. You just do what you have to do."

Though I don't like it, he's right. I have enough to deal with here. I have to trust that Bastion won't let our dad get in any deeper than he already is.

A weary feeling sets in my bones. Will this be the rest of my existence? Forever trying to keep my father from doom of his own making?

"You want a drink?" Bastion asks, getting up out of his chair.

"Just a beer."

He walks to the bar, and when I glance over, I see that it's taken him about fifteen seconds to flirt with the bartender. No surprise there. Bastion is a charmer. It's part of what makes him so successful in running scams.

He returns a couple of minutes later and slides a bottle of beer in front of me before taking his seat. He lifts his beer to his lips. "So, what's your new boss like?"

I shrug, picking at the label on the beer bottle. "A bit of a dick. It's clear he doesn't want me there, but I can handle him."

"What the hell does a billionaire have to be a dick about?" Bastion shakes his head and takes another swig of his drink.

"Who knows, and who cares. I just need to stick it out long enough to pay off Dad's debt." I don't want to talk about Obsidian Voss anymore. He's on my mind enough as it is. "How's it going with your lady love?"

Bastion sets his beer on the table and grins. "Good. She got me an expensive watch for our three-month anniversary."

"How come you're not wearing it?" I bring the beer to my lips.

"Sold it. Can't let you take all the glory, you know." He winks.

The warmth that hits my heart because he's helping me says how fucked up a childhood we had. But Bastion has my back, and he always will.

"What are you going to say when she asks where it is?"

He lifts his beer off the table. "Gonna say it's too nice to wear, makes me nervous I'm going to lose it. Then I'm going to tell her the house was broken into, and someone stole it."

"You think she'll buy it?" I'm doubtful, but who knows? Bastion is really that good.

"She will when I distract her with my face between her legs." He laughs while I wrinkle my nose in disgust.

"Gross." I take a large draw from my beer. The last thing I want to think about is the reason why Bastion is so successful in siphoning off rich women's money.

We chat for a while about other stuff, and I notice Bastion's gaze flicking over my shoulder a few times during our conversation.

"What are you looking at?" I look over my shoulder.

"A bunch of SUVs keep rolling through town. They all look the same—black, blacked-out windows, expensive. What's with that?"

I turn to face him again and shrug. "No idea."

The bartender comes over—probably because there aren't a lot of people here tonight, and she wants more attention from Bastion. "Did you two want another round?"

"Hey, sweetheart, what's with all those SUVs driving through town?"

The easy-going expression on her face dies and tension fills her frame. Her gaze darts around the bar. "They're all coming from the private airport. Headed up to Midnight Manor for the night."

Bastion frowns. "What's Midnight Manor?"

"Where the Voss brothers live," she whispers as though if she says their name too loudly, they might appear out of thin air with pickaxes.

Bastion's gaze flicks over to me for a second. "What happens up there?"

She shrugs. "No one knows. But it happens on the last Saturday of every month." She glances around again, then straightens to her full height. "Did you want another round?"

"Sure thing, sweetheart. Thanks," Bastion says as casually as if they were talking about the weather. He really is impressive with his ability to be inconspicuous.

She nods and heads back behind the bar.

As soon as she's gone, his gaze turns serious at me. "What's the deal with the SUVs?"

I shrug. "I have no idea. First I've heard of it."

"Is it a party or some shit?" His eyes bore into me as if I'm lying to him.

"I just told you I don't know."

He continues to look out the window as another tinted SUV goes by. "You need to figure it out."

I want to argue with him, but I can't. Even more valuable than what's in my bag is information. And whatever goes on up at Midnight Manor, it's clearly not common knowledge, which means it's being kept a mystery on purpose.

Information I could use to blackmail the brothers, but I have to find out what the mystery is first.

The bartender delivers our beers to the table, and Bastion pulls out a twenty, telling her to keep the change. She thanks him with a smile and returns to the bar.

"I'll see what I can find out. Let's finish these beers so I can get back to the manor and poke around."

We finish in record time and make our way out of the bar. I follow Bastion to the rental car he parked in the side lot, and we go around to the far side of the car. He unlocks the door and pulls a bag out of the passenger seat, holding it open. After making sure no one is around, I carefully remove the Fabergé egg from my purse and set it inside the bag.

Bastion looks inside the bag. "What the fuck am I supposed to do with an egg?"

I narrow my eyes. "You know what to do with it. That thing is worth a small fortune."

"Why didn't you take jewelry? Something easier to get rid of?"

"Jewelry is too risky. Someone will notice right away that it's missing."

He begrudgingly nods.

Another blacked-out SUV passes by, headed toward Midnight Manor. I fish my phone out of my purse and text the driver to let him know I'm ready to be picked up. I was given a phone by Voss Enterprises for my job, but I message

Bastion through my personal phone because I'm sure the one supplied by them is monitored.

"I'll see you next Saturday. Keep Dad out of trouble." I give Bastion a hug.

"I will. You stay out of trouble, too." He looked to where the SUV was headed. "You know what Dad says—those people aren't like us. They have no loyalty and can't be trusted, so watch your back."

I don't bother arguing with Bastion that Dad could use his own lesson in loyalty and not screwing over his kin. It was a tenant of our upbringing—we are not like them.

"I'll be careful." I hike my purse higher on my shoulder and step away to wait on the porch of the bar for my ride.

I'd been looking forward to relaxing when I got back to the manor, maybe going for a late-night swim in the pool, but it seems I have a mystery to solve.

Exactly what are the Vosses hiding at Midnight Manor? I'll find out.

CHAPTER

TEN

ARIANA

When the driver approaches the house, there's no sign of the SUVs that were supposedly headed here, which seems odd. Where could they all be?

I act as though nothing is amiss and thank the mute driver for picking me up. I walk through the front door and listen until I hear him drive away, presumably to park the car wherever they go when they're not in service, then I sneak back outside.

There are ways to access the outside from the inside of the manor, but I don't have the layout memorized yet, so it will be easier to just make my way around the behemoth estate until I figure out where all the SUVs went.

I get lucky because there's barely any moon tonight and fog hangs on the ground, so it's easy for me to creep along the edge of the building. There's only the odd sconce here and there around the manor, and even then, their flickering light seems to be absorbed by the night.

I walk for at least fifteen minutes, and just when I'm starting to think that my efforts are futile, I hear the crunch of tires on gravel. I jump behind a bush beside the manor and peek out.

A black SUV passes by on a thin path to my left that I didn't notice since it's so dark out. Once it's out of sight, I listen, and when I hear nothing, I come out from behind the bush and keep walking toward where it was headed. Every sound makes me jump. I'm paranoid I'm going to find myself in a set of headlights.

My body grows tense as I round the corner of one of the turrets, but a quiet squeal falls from my lips when I spot SUVs parked off in the distance. I slowly make my way closer, careful to stay close to the dark stone of the manor. When I'm as close as I dare to go, I settle in behind greenery and watch.

A large door is open on the side of the manor, and low light shines from somewhere inside.

The sound of a vehicle door opening pierces the night, and I take note of all the SUVs until I see a woman with a black mask get out of the back seat of one of the cars and make her way toward the door. She's wearing what I think is a costume, though that seems weird since it's not even close to October. It looks as if maybe she's supposed to be an angel because there are little white wings on her back when she passes through the door. But her costume is more like lingerie than an actual costume.

I'm not sure what to make of it, nor of the burly men on either side of the door standing guard. It's obvious this is a private event, and that even if I did have the balls to sneak in and see what's going on, I wouldn't make it past those guys. And if they're all wearing costumes, I'd stand out.

The two guys in question close the door and remain as sentries outside. I watch for a while longer, but no one else comes or goes, so I eventually return the way I came and go back in the manor through the front door.

I get lost trying to make it to the east wing, and I can't help feeling watched. Every time I pass a painting, I assume it must be some long-lost Voss ancestor. If I believed in eerie, unexplained things, I'd swear they were watching me.

When I finally reach the long, arched hallway that leads to the east wing, I pause in front of the stained-glass picture of a wolf. It's clearly no coincidence that this leads to Obsidian's private area, and he has a wolf tattoo on his neck. It must have some meaning, but I don't know what.

The day I arrived and met Asher in person, I noticed he had a bear tattoo on one of his hands. There's more to these Voss brothers than meets the eye.

I continue on my way, staying in the middle of the hallway that leads to my room so I remain out of the shadows cast by the sconces on the walls. I'm not even sure why. It just feels safer somehow.

I get ready for bed, and once I'm finally tucked under the covers with the lights off, sleep is hard to find. My mind is preoccupied with what is happening at the manor tonight.

Why was the woman wearing a mask? Why was she dressed as a sexy angel?

Why are presumably rich people flying into the private airport to come here once a month?

Why does nobody in town know what's going on?

Eventually, I drift off, but I'm no closer to the truth.

I don't know what wakes me, but I snap into a sitting position.

It's no longer fully dark outside, but it's not fully morning either. The first signs of dawn make themselves known. Birds chirp outside the arched Gothic windows, and the smallest hint of daylight shines in the horizon.

When I glance around the room for some idea of what woke me from a dead sleep, something on the floor catches my eye. I frown and slide out of bed, crouching. It looks like a trail of... I run my fingers over it... sand.

What the hell?

Straightening, I follow the trail with my gaze and see that it leads to my closed bedroom door. I walk alongside it and open my door. It continues down the hall as far as I can see.

Equal parts intrigued and confused, I follow the trail until it leads to a door that goes outside. Glancing around then down at myself still in my underwear and oversized T-shirt that I wore to bed, I decide that since no one's around, I'll keep following the trail. It's so early, and it's Sunday, so I doubt anyone is wandering around outside.

I follow the sand some distance from the manor to where it looks like it stops dead in front of an ivy-covered stone wall, but as I draw nearer, I realize there's actually an arched iron gate in the wall that's also covered with ivy, and the line of sand continues past it.

I pause with my hand on the iron gate, part of me questioning whether I should go any farther. I mean, what is this? Who would have laid a trail of sand to lead me all this way and why? How did they get into my room without me hearing them?

But something pulls me forward and has me pushing open the creaking iron gate. A few steps inside, and I realize I'm entering a gorgeous walled-off garden. A look down the length of it reveals statues set in ivy along the perimeter of the high stone wall, flower gardens throughout, and trellises with climbing flowers covering them over a few of the pathways that lead to the center fountain.

It's like a hidden paradise.

"What the hell are you doing?"

I whip around with a startled gasp. Obsidian's eyes are black as night, staring at me with an intensity so fierce I struggle not to run away from not only here but the manor completely.

"I... I..." I glance to the side to motion to the trail of sand that led me here, but I double-take, spinning all the way around. "It's gone." I blink several times, trying to make sense of how sand could somehow disappear without one grain visible.

"What's gone?"

"Um…" I'll sound like an idiot if I say I followed an imaginary path of sand that led me right to him. "Nothing. Sorry."

He narrows his eyes and brings a joint to his lips, taking a pull off it. Deep, dark circles hang under his eyes, and his clothes are rumpled. His wavy hair on top looks mussed as though he's run his fingers through it a thousand times. Despite all of that, he's still the most attractive man I've ever seen in person.

"I couldn't sleep," I say.

"That doesn't explain why you're out here at the crack of dawn, looking like you just rolled out of bed."

His gaze drops to my legs, and I remember that I'm standing in front of my boss sans bra or pants in only an oversized T-shirt. I pull at the hem of the shirt, trying to cover up.

"Don't do that on my account. I'm enjoying the view." He takes another pull off the joint, then tosses it on the ground and crushes it beneath his shoe.

"I didn't think I'd see anyone. It's so early." I glance at the sky where the first tendrils of daylight are making an appearance.

Without a word, he walks over to a bench set to the side of the path. He flops down into it and leans back, legs spread and chin up, face pointed at the sky. Gone is his usual suave nature. There's something forlorn about his presence.

Getting the hell out of here would probably be smart, but for some reason, I can't make my bare feet move. Instead, I walk toward Obsidian, although tentatively. He's the definition of a closed book, but something in my gut tugs me his way.

"What are you doing here? Have you been up all night?"

He lifts his head to look at me when I come to stand in front of him. "That obvious?"

I shrug. "Kinda. You on a bender?"

He chuckles low in his throat, but there's no humor there. "I wish. No, nothing like that." Obsidian heaves out a sigh, and it sounds so tired, so sad, that I draw closer.

"Are you all right?"

Seeing a man as powerful as him like this is strange. The Obsidian who showed up in his office all week was a five-foot-thick concrete wall, like nothing could pierce his exterior. But the man in front of me this morning is so far removed from that persona. Somehow, I instinctively know that the man here this morning is the one I saved from drowning on that beach.

He doesn't answer my question. He just continues to stare at me.

"Do you want me to leave?" I ask when the silence stretches too thin.

He slowly shakes his head, never taking his eyes off me. "I don't want to be alone."

I nod. We're quiet for another few beats until I think of something to say. "What is this place?" I gesture to the garden surrounding us.

"You've never seen a garden before?"

My head tilts and my mouth presses into a thin line. He might be feeling low, but clearly not all remnants of the man who likes to push my buttons have disappeared. "Obviously, but this seems like more than just a garden."

He frowns for a second. "My mom used to call it the secret garden when we were young."

His gaze drifts to somewhere behind me, and he remains fixated on it. I turn around to see what he might be looking at, but I see nothing but a flower garden that looks like all the others.

"Did you spend a lot of time here?" Maybe it's somewhere he likes to go when he wants to clear his head.

Obsidian shakes his head. "Not back then. More these days."

He's not giving me much to work with, but at least he's talking to me without trying to be the world's biggest dick. Progress.

"It's really beautiful." I turn to look around the garden once more, but when I face him again, his gaze is roaming my body.

My cheeks heat, and I resist the urge to press my thighs together.

What would it be like to sleep with a man like Obsidian? I've only ever been with guys around my own age. Something tells me that being with Obsidian would be an experience that's worlds away from any I've had. No part of me can picture him making love or being gentle in bed. He probably fucks all his partners like an animal exerting his dominance.

I stifle a groan at that thought.

He straightens on the bench and leans forward, resting his forearms on his thighs. "It pales in comparison to you."

My eyes widen, and my breath picks up. It's the first compliment he's given me, and the sexual tension goes into overdrive. Does he mean it? Is he setting me up for some cruel joke so he can laugh at me later?

"You've got great legs." His knuckles skim along the side of my leg, coming to rest on my hip, under my T-shirt.

I suck in a breath, knowing I should back away but somehow unable to.

He waits for my reaction, fixated on me. When I don't move, his eyes glitter, knowing I decided not to move, and he squeezes my hip. The heat of his skin on mine spreads through my body like a spiderweb.

"They're distracting when you wear a skirt or a dress." His voice is as rough as the stone beneath my feet.

"Is that why you're such an asshole to me?" The words slip out of my mouth.

A deep chuckle leaves his lips. "No, that's just because my brothers think I need a babysitter, and you were chosen for the job. It's nothing personal."

I'd gathered as much, but it still doesn't mean it's easy to set aside.

He moves the hand on my hip, sliding it around to my back and over the globe of my ass. He squeezes and groans. "Fuck, this ass is distracting as fuck too."

I don't dare move, afraid to break the spell, loving the feel of his hands on me.

But then I remember what I'm here to do, and when his hand slides again, his fingers coming close to the crack of my ass, I abruptly step back.

Anger flashes across his face, and his gaze meets mine.

"I should go." I don't wait for him to say anything as I scurry toward the iron gate I came through, all the while attempting to hold my T-shirt down enough that it covers my ass. Not my most graceful exit to be sure.

It doesn't matter though. I need some space from Obsidian because the last thing I can do is become even more attracted to him. I'm here for one purpose only, and it's not to fall for the billionaire bad boy, no matter what games he's playing.

CHAPTER

ELEVEN

OBSIDIAN

"She needs to go." I push a hand through my hair as I pace in front of Asher's desk on Monday morning.

"Is she incapable of doing her job?" he asks, hands steepled in front of him, rocking back in his chair.

I wish that were the case. It would make it easy to get rid of her. Asher doesn't tolerate incompetence. None of us do. But she's fucking good at her job, unfortunately. She anticipates what I need before I can even ask for it, and everything I assigned her last week was done correctly with efficiency. There's no question that she's taken a lot off my plate, and it has been helpful in relieving some of that pressure.

"That's not it. I told you. I don't need a babysitter." I turn to face him, hoping he'll buy the lie.

It's true, I don't need someone watching over me and reporting back to my brothers if that's what she's doing,

97

but that's not why Ariana has to go. It's because she's a goddamn siren, and the pull to her grows stronger by the day.

I was fucked up on alcohol and weed when I ran into her in the garden yesterday, and I've almost convinced myself that's the only reason I allowed myself to touch her and call her beautiful. But now that I know what her bare skin feels like beneath my palm, it's even harder to keep my head in check. I tossed and turned in bed all night, imagining what it would be like to fuck her the way I want to—insatiable and primal. To make her bend to my will and push her past her comfort zone.

"She's not a babysitter, Sid. I know you think we probably have her reporting back to us, but that's not the case."

Pressing my hands against the desk, I lean toward him. "Why'd you hire her specifically?" Did he somehow know that she'd get under my skin?

"She didn't seem like she'd take your shit. That's what I liked about her." He shrugs.

He's not wrong. Ariana barely bats an eye when I'm a dick to her. Either that or she comes back at me, but always with a smile on her face and always in a way that's not quite direct enough for me to call her out.

"Exactly. My assistant should have respect for me. She should not be constantly challenging me."

"Is that what you call it when a woman doesn't let you put her in her place?"

Anabelle's voice from behind me causes me to straighten and face her.

"That's not what this is about," I tell her.

"Isn't it though?" She rises off her chair and makes her way to Asher, bending to give him a chaste kiss.

He tugs her into his lap. Their display of such easy affection makes my chest tighten, knowing it's not something I'm ever destined for.

"You know, I've been thinking," Anabelle says. "Maybe Ariana should dine with us in the dining room rather than always eating alone in her room."

I narrow my eyes at my sister-in-law. "That's not happening."

Asher chuckles. "If I didn't know better, I'd say there's some other reason you're so worked up about this woman."

"Fuck off." I turn and start out of his office. "Thanks for nothing."

I prowl from his office and make my way to the east wing. When I arrive at my office, I stand at the threshold, watching as Ariana bends over, fussing with the shredder beside her desk.

It takes everything in me to bite back the groan that wants to crawl up my throat because she's wearing a tight skirt that hits above her knee. Now that she's bending over, her shapely legs are on display, as is that perfect ass of hers.

Drawing in a deep breath, I step past the threshold and don't say a word as I make my way over to my desk. It's as if I can feel her attention shift from what she's doing to me. It feels like a caress with a light hand over the skin on my neck, and I'd bet good money on the fact that she's eyeing the tattoo there.

"Did you pull all the files for the Enersync buyout like I asked?" I use my mouse to turn on my computer screen and type in my password. Only once I'm logged in do I turn my gaze to her.

Her luscious red hair is pulled away from her face, and it somehow makes her look even younger than her twenty-four years. She's fresh-faced and exudes innocence today, which unfortunately only makes me want her more.

Ariana stares at me for a beat, almost as though she's waiting for me to say something else. Something about me putting my hands on her yesterday morning? Not happening. If she's smart, she'll read that I'm going to play this like nothing ever happened, and she will too.

She seems to reach that conclusion and clears her throat, then lifts her chin a bit. "I did. Uploaded them to the cloud in their own folder. If you want anything printed, let me know. The emails that need your attention are on the corner of your desk, and your two o'clock Zoom meeting had to move it up to one, so I changed that on your calendar."

I don't bother saying thanks, just turn back to my computer.

"Did you want to dictate your response to the emails?" she asks after a moment.

"No, I'll respond to them myself." I don't trust myself to be any closer to her and not jump over my desk and pounce on her.

My phone buzzes with a text, and I see that Mr. Smith sent me a message.

> No luck tracking down the girl from the beach. Seems to be a dead end. I can keep trying if you want.

My mouth twists to the side. I'm not even sure what I hope to accomplish by tracking down the woman who saved my life. But I can't get the vision of that locket hanging in front of my face out of my head, or that singing, though I'm not sure it's even hers. But something keeps tugging on me to find out who she is.

But what the hell am I going to do? If Mr. Smith can't find her, she can't be found.

> Never mind then. Call it off. I'll send your payment today.

Setting down my phone, I push what happened on the beach from my mind. I don't need something else on my mind. It's best to let it go.

We work quietly for a couple of hours, and I stifle a groan of frustration when I receive a text from a colleague about an event I'm supposed to attend next week. One that Ariana will have to attend with me. I wish I could blow it off, but it's imperative for Voss Enterprises that I be there to represent our interests and shore up support for our position.

"We're going to be traveling for a few days next week. Someone at the head office will take care of the arrangements, but you'll need to make sure you have the proper attire."

She swivels around in her chair to face me, and I force my gaze not to dip down to her bare legs. "Where will we be going?"

It's possible that she looks as horrified at having to spend time alone outside of the estate as I feel.

"Washington, DC."

She nods. "What type of events will we be attending? Is what I normally wear insufficient?"

"Your cheap polyester skirts won't cut it. And we have a fundraiser ball to go to. Talk to Marcel, and he can get you something that doesn't look like it came from Walmart." I'm deliberately cruel to make her want even less to do with me.

I steel myself against the flash of hurt that shines in her blue eyes, holding her gaze and daring her to say something. But she only nods, and weirdly, I find myself disappointed that she didn't come back at me. Tell me what a rich prick I sound like and that not everyone is born into money.

"I'll make sure to talk to him about it today," she says before she turns back around to her desk.

Why do I feel an impending sense of doom like no matter what I do or how mean I am, nothing is going to change the fact that I'm drawn to the woman in this room with me?

There may be a constant lonely ache inside me, but that doesn't mean that I want to fill it. Despite how I might act, I don't want to hurt anyone. The idea of being what my father was to my mother is utterly soul-destroying to me.

And if there's one thing I'm sure of, it's that I'm becoming more like my father than ever.

MY MOOD DETERIORATED as the week progressed. Basically, the more I found myself wanting Ariana, the bigger a dick I became. She never said anything, though, quietly going about her duties and making herself infuriatingly indispensable.

It's Saturday night, and yesterday she told me that Marcel had acquired her clothing for our trip. Ever since then, I've been imagining what she might bring with her. She's been running a fashion show in my mind, and with every hour that passes, the articles of clothing get smaller and smaller, more and more see-through.

I fist my hand and bring it to my mouth, groaning. This needs to stop. I know it does. But if that's the case, why the fuck am I home on a Saturday night? I could easily make a few calls, take the jet to a nearby city, and work her out of my system with someone else. There are more than a few women who are willing and able. But for some reason, the idea doesn't appeal in the least.

So here I am, walking down the hall to Ariana's room, making up a bullshit fucking excuse to see her—like wanting to make sure what she has for our trip is appropriate.

I rap loudly on her bedroom door. I hear no movement from behind the door, and when she doesn't answer, I knock again. Louder this time. Screw her if she's trying to avoid me.

Once again, she doesn't answer the door, so I try the handle, and the door opens.

"Ariana?" I step inside. "Ariana?"

It smells like her in here—like a tropical beach. The ocean.

With sure steps, I check the en suite and the walk-in closet and find both empty. It's not as though I keep track of her coming and going, but where could she have gone?

I leave her room in search of Marcel, who always knows what's going on within Midnight Manor. I find him speaking to Finn, his boyfriend. Finn's in charge of the housekeeping staff in the manor.

Marcel straightens when he sees me. "Sir, can I assist you with something?"

I give a nod to Finn in greeting. "Do you know where Ariana is?"

"I'm not exactly sure, but she did ask me to have one of the drivers take her into town. I can check with him if you like."

"Please."

I wait while Marcel calls the driver on his cell phone, and after a brief conversation, he hangs up and slides the phone back into his pocket. "He said he dropped Miss Clarke off at Black Magic Bar. Apparently, it's the same place she went last Saturday night."

There's no helping the frown that tilts my lips down. What the hell is she doing in a dive bar? Is she there to pick someone up for the night?

My hands fist at my sides at that thought. "Thank you, Marcel."

Without even attempting to stop myself, I head straight for the front door, grabbing my car keys as I go, and slip into my Rolls Royce.

CHAPTER

TWELVE

ARIANA

On Saturday night, the driver once again drops me off in front of Black Magic Bar.

The guilt felt like tar on my skin as I slid the solid gold figurine into my bag before leaving Midnight Manor. I actually felt sick to my stomach. But I reminded myself that my dad and brother are counting on me and forced myself not to put it back.

Bastion is sitting at the same table as last week, and the bartender is leaning against it while he flirts with her. His gaze flicks in my direction, and she looks over her shoulder at me. She straightens when she sees me, looking mildly chastised.

I hang my bag on the back of the chair and chuckle. "Relax, he's my brother, not my boyfriend."

Her cheeks glow pink. "Can I get you guys anything?"

"A whiskey on ice for me," I say, sitting across from Bastion.

"Beer for me," he says to her with a wink.

Her pink cheeks flare, and she nods, walking over to the bar.

"Whiskey?" He arches an eyebrow. "Rough week?"

I blow out a breath. "Sort of. My boss is really riding my ass this week. It's getting harder to grin and bear it."

"Well, it's not forever, at least."

I nod. "You able to get rid of that thing from last week?" I glance around to see if anyone is paying us any attention, but they're all doing their own thing.

He grins. "Hell yeah. That shit was worth some major money, Ari, good job."

When he tells me how much he got for it, my eyes widen, and the elation is mixed with that oily feeling inside me that what I'm doing is wrong.

I nod, wanting to change the topic. "You able to keep Dad in check?"

Bastion rolls his eyes. "Stop worrying about Dad, would you? You worry about what you're here for, and I'll worry about what's going on at home."

He's right, but it's hard when I know my father to be his own worst enemy. "Fine."

The bartender delivers our drinks, and Bastion looks around to make sure we won't be overheard before he asks his next question. "You case a bunch of things this week while you were there?"

I shrug. "Yeah, I have a mental list of what I think will be easy to take without being noticed."

He grins as though I said I robbed a bank. "Awesome. See, this is why you should have never left the family business."

I scowl. "Don't get any ideas. As soon as this is all settled for Dad, that's it for me... again. This isn't the life I want for myself."

Bastion scoffs and takes a pull from his drink. "Are you kidding me? You feeling sorry for some fucking billionaires, Ari? Give me a break. It's assholes like that who have ruined the world for the rest of us. You know that."

Dad's brainwashing has worked on Bastion, for sure.

"Maybe you should try to think for yourself sometimes, Bast, before you eat up everything Dad says. His way of thinking hasn't exactly led him to a good spot in his life."

Bastion blinks several times, mouth gaping. "What the hell is going on with you?"

I lean over the table. "You know I want no part of this kind of thing anymore."

He shakes his head, studying me. "No... there's something more." He pauses for a beat. "Ari, tell me you're not falling for this guy or something. You don't have feelings for him, do you?"

I scoff, though I can't help but feel that's exactly what's happening. Maybe not feelings exactly, but I sure as hell am drawn to him on a physical level. The fact that we have to go away together next week has been weighing on me.

What will it be like to be on a private plane with him? A hotel? I know we're not staying in the same room, but still. He and I will be in a different environment, including a ball. I don't know anything about attending a ball.

I have to admit that Obsidian's comment about my cheap clothing hit a tender spot inside of me, though I hid it. Will it be obvious that I've never attended anything like a ball before? That I don't know how to dance?

"I don't have feelings for him. The guy is a royal prick. Give me a break, Bast." I lift my drink and only allow myself a small sip. A large one will confirm to him I'm full of shit.

He studies me for a beat but says, "Good. Keep it that way."

I roll my eyes. "Fill me in on what's going on with your lady love."

Bastion accepts my change of subject, and we chat for the next couple of hours, until he has to go so that he can catch the red-eye back west. He pays the tab at the bar, and we leave together, going out to the side lot where his rental car was last week.

Once again, I pass him the item I stole from Midnight Manor, and he puts it in his own bag and sets it in the passenger seat.

"Should I be worried about you? You seem a little off." He pulls me in for a hug, and I go willingly.

"I'm fine, Bast. I swear." I squeeze him back. As much as I wanted some separation from him and my father, I'm real-izing how much I'd miss Bastion if he weren't in my life.

I'm still in his embrace when headlights hit us from the side. I squint and pull away, trying to cover my eyes with my hand to make out who it is and why they're shining their lights at us.

"What the fuck?" Bastion grumbles.

I can't make anything out, but I hear the car door open, then the silhouette of a man breaks through the beams of light. When he gets closer, I suck in a breath, realizing it's Obsidian.

Shit. He caught me. I knew a place like Midnight Manor probably had cameras, but I looked and couldn't find any. Figured it was because they never have outsiders here so what was the point. I'm sure I didn't miss any, so did someone see me?

Rage and fury morph every aristocratic feature on Obsidian's face.

"What are you doing here?" I ask.

"Could ask you the same thing," he growls.

My stomach swoops like a bird diving down from the sky. "I didn't call for a ride back yet." I sound like a nervous, blubbering idiot.

"I'm your ride. Get in the fucking car."

Bastion steps forward and opens his mouth to say something, but I turn and widen my eyes at him, giving him a look that tells him to keep his mouth shut.

"It's fine, Bast. I've got this," I say in a low voice.

Bastion's hands fist at his sides and his jaw clenches, but he gives me a tight nod. "Text me and let me know you get home okay."

"Will do." I give him a wan smile and walk over to the passenger side of Obsidian's vehicle.

With my hand on the door handle, I wait while Obsidian stares down my brother as if he wishes actual lasers would fire out of his eyes. Only when he walks back toward the car do I open the door and slide inside.

Normally, I'd take a moment to sit in awe of this vehicle that's worth hundreds of thousands of dollars, but I'm too nervous to gawk. Obsidian slams the car door closed once he's inside and peels in reverse out of the parking lot. I do my best to give Bastion a reassuring look that all is well, though I don't believe it myself. But we both can't be in jail.

What would make Obsidian this angry except knowing I've been stealing from him?

Figuring silence is the best course of action, I don't say anything as he drives recklessly. But when he passes the turnoff to Midnight Manor, I stiffen in my seat, wondering where he might be taking me. Is he going to drive me to the police station? Maybe it wasn't only Uma I had to be scared of.

I pull at the hem of my dress, wishing I'd worn something other than a cute little sundress tonight. But it was so sweltering when I left, I couldn't fathom wearing anything else, and Black Magic doesn't have air conditioning.

Obsidian tracks my movement, and his gaze goes to my legs before he looks back at the road and increases his speed. My heart races as I watch the speedometer go up. It's danger-ous, and though we may be on country roads late at night, if anyone pulled out in front of us, there would be no chance of us avoiding a collision.

"Aren't you going a little fast?" I ask breathlessly, my chest tight from the anxiety this car ride is giving me.

"Shut up!" he shouts, glancing at me briefly. His dark eyes are filled with anguish and irritation.

When he takes a corner so fast that I'm afraid the door might pop open, and I'll roll out of the car, I grip his arm. Despite my fear, I can't help but notice the hard muscles underneath his expensive dress shirt. "Mr. Voss, slow down. You're scaring me."

"Good! Seems to be a fair exchange because you drive me fucking crazy!" He punches the steering wheel with the arm I'm not holding onto.

I stare at him wide-eyed. It's alarming to see this man who is normally so put together and in control of his emotions, even if it's anger or irritation, unraveled. My hand drops from his arm.

"Who was that guy I caught you with?"

"Caught me? What do you mean *caught* me? That implies there's something between us, and newsflash, Mr. Voss, you are my boss and nothing more."

At least he slows down the car a little at my angry outburst.

His head whips in my direction. "Is that right?" There's a challenge in his voice.

"Yes! What I do with my personal time is of no consequence to you. It's none of your business."

His deep chuckle fills the car. "Do you actually believe that, or like me, is that some lie you're trying to trick yourself into believing?"

My lips press together in a thin line. "I said what I said. It's not your business who he was. You're just my boss, and I'm off the clock."

I don't know why I don't tell him that Bastion is my brother, but I don't want to. Pride or defiance or maybe just being sick of taking his shit for the past two weeks.

His hand sails over the console between the seats until he's cupping my pussy over my underwear. I suck in a breath, but to my own shame, I don't push his hand away because it feels good. It feels *right*.

With wide eyes, I look where his hand disappears underneath my sundress, then look at him. My heart is a commanding bass drum in my chest, so loud I swear he must be able to hear it.

"Feel how fucking hot and wet you are... are you telling me this is for him, not me?" he growls, still looking at the road.

"It's not for him," I nearly whisper.

"Who is he?" He grips my mound tighter, then spares me a look before returning his attention to the road. "Who. Is. He?"

"None of your business."

A deep sadistic chuckle leaves his lips. "I'm going to get it out of you. Now tell me who he is to you."

This is a battle of wills I'm determined to win. "No."

Obsidian lifts his hand, and I think that he'll pull away. The weight of my disappointment at that thought should probably concern me. Instead, he slips his hand under the waistband of my underwear, and his finger brushes my clit.

I bite my lip, stifling the moan that wants to escape my lips, but my legs widen in supplication, so it's obvious to him I want more.

"Who is he?" He dips his fingers lower and pushes one finger into me, then uses the heel of his palm to apply pressure to my clit at the same time.

My head falls back against the headrest, and my eyes close, my moan slipping out.

"Tell me who he is, Ariana. I want to know." He adds another finger, stretching me in the most delicious way.

Eyes still closed, I shake my head.

He continues to work me, asking over and over who Bastion is.

My head lolls to the side, and I watch his profile while he works me with one hand and the steering wheel with his other. He's focused, lasered in on his goal, all power and dominance, and I can't help but wonder what it would be like to fully give myself to a man like Obsidian.

Would he care for me and help me discover heights I never knew existed, or would he destroy me?

We're driving too fast, his attention half on what he's doing to me and half on the dark road in front of us, but I can't find it in myself to care. I'm barreling toward an orgasm of epic proportions, and that's all that matters.

He pulls his fingers from me and centers all his attention on my clit. My insides contract as I draw closer to an orgasm.

"Tell me who he is."

My back arches off the seat, and I groan.

Obsidian looks at me, eyes black as midnight. "Only good girls get to come, Ariana. Are you going to tell me who he is?"

I almost slip. I almost let the words fall from my mouth, but I won't satisfy him. "No."

He increases the pressure on my clit until I'm at the brink, one second from crumbling. Then he yanks his hands from between my legs, and I groan. "Then you don't get to come."

A wounded animal cry whips from my throat. "No!"

"Tell me who he is, and I'll let you finish."

What a prick.

He flicks his gaze at me with a self-satisfied smirk, probably thinking he's got me. *Not today, asshole.*

I bring my own hand between my legs and rub circles over my clit.

His hands tighten on the steering wheel. He's obviously displeased, but at the same time, he keeps peeking at me, jaw tight. His foot presses on the gas until I'm pushed back into the seat by the force, and I come on a cry, rocking my hips into my hand as I reach my peak.

It's not as satisfying as if he'd made me come, but it's enough to relieve the ache.

Obsidian says nothing as I catch my breath.

"Bastion is my brother."

His body tenses then relaxes.

We don't speak the rest of the drive back to Midnight Manor, and when he drops me off in front of the door, then races off into the night in his expensive car, I do my best not to worry about how this changes things.

CHAPTER

THIRTEEN

OBSIDIAN

I pull the vehicle to a stop in front of the hotel in Washington, DC, trying not to think of the last time I was driving a vehicle with Ariana as the passenger, though those images have been circling my brain constantly during the couple of days that have passed.

That woman shocked the hell out of me when she finished herself off after I refused to. She's fucking stubborn. Why wouldn't she just tell me the guy was her brother when I first asked?

Because you were an asshole about it.

There's more to Ariana than meets the eye, that much is obvious.

We haven't talked about what happened. It's almost as though we're playing a game of chicken, and the first one to bring it up loses.

The valet comes to collect the keys for the car I had waiting at the private airport for us, while another opens Ariana's door.

"Leave everything in the car. They'll bring it up," I tell her as I walk past.

Today she's wearing a navy skirt and a white sleeveless blouse. Though there's nothing inherently sexy about the outfit, she looks sexy in it. The expensive fabric falls over her curves to perfection, and it's never been more obvious that this woman belongs in a better lifestyle than the one she's been afforded.

The manager meets me in the lobby, as always. This is a Voss Enterprises property after all.

"Good afternoon, Mr. Voss. The suite is ready for you." He hands me two key cards for the presidential suite.

"Thank you, Rory. This is Ariana Clarke." I motion to Ariana at my side. "She's my personal assistant. Anything she asks for is like getting a directive from me, clear?"

He looks at Ariana and nods, giving her a polite smile. I can see the curiosity on his face since I've never been here with anyone else while conducting business. "Of course, sir. Pleasure to meet you."

"Have our bags brought up and have a charcuterie tray as well as two steak dinners sent to the suite. You know how I like mine, and medium well for Miss Clarke. Some light refreshments too."

"Right away, sir." With swift efficiency, Rory turns on his heel and goes off to accommodate my request.

"Let's go." I don't wait for Ariana to acknowledge my order.

Ever since Saturday night, my skin feels too tight every time I'm around her. It's impossible to be in her vicinity and not think of her slick heat and the way she clenched around my fingers.

I stab the button for the elevator harder than necessary, and we wait in silence until it dings and the doors open. Being the gentleman I am, I motion for Ariana to go first.

Once we're inside and moving up, she turns to me. "Why did he say suite and not rooms? Emphasis on the plural."

I turn my head toward her. "Because we're staying in the presidential suite. Don't worry, there's more than one bedroom."

I should have booked her a room of her own. It would have been the smart thing to do—to put some distance between us. Maybe bring home one of my regulars to fuck and take the edge off. But I didn't want to give her the opportunity to do the same with some asshat she might meet at the hotel bar.

She doesn't say anything, nor does she speak when the elevator doors part on the top floor, and I lead us down the hall to our suite. I open the door and gesture for her to go in first.

"Wow." Ariana takes a few steps inside, then stops and turns, taking in the space. "I've never been in a room this nice before."

She seems to think better of sharing that with me. Her gaze flies to mine, and her cheeks deepen in color.

"Not many people have." Usually, I'd be a prick about it. Say something to make her even more uncomfortable. But for some reason, the impulse is easy to crush. I step past her. "I'll be staying in that room." I point at the bedroom door to my left. "There are two other bedrooms on this side of the suite. Take whichever one you'd like."

She goes from one room to the next, taking her time looking inside. When she reappears, she points at the door on her right. "I'm going to take that one. It has a better view."

Just then, there's a knock on the door, so I step over and find that it's the bellhop. I direct him to which bedroom each piece of luggage should go, and before he leaves, I slip him a hundred-dollar bill.

"You'll want to unpack and get settled, I'm sure, but do it quickly. It won't take long for the steaks to arrive." I walk toward my bedroom, needing some space from her.

Temptation can only be pushed aside for so long. I'm not a fucking saint.

I quickly unpack my things and change out of my suit into a pair of lounge pants and a T-shirt. After, I make my way out to the living area and turn on the TV, changing it to the business news. There's another knock at the door, and an attendant rolls a cart into the suite with our food on it.

"Just put it over there." I direct him to leave it near the dining room table and tip him before he leaves. "Ariana, food's here."

I lift the silver domes from the plates to ensure we've been delivered what I asked for. There's no response, so I walk over to the closed door of her bedroom and knock.

"Ariana." I heave a sigh when once again she doesn't answer. "What the fuck is she doing in there?" I knock again, but she still doesn't answer.

Did something happen? Did she leave the suite while I was in my bedroom? Did she have some medical event and is lying helplessly on the floor? A hundred thoughts whizz through my head.

I turn the handle to the door and swing it open, stilling at what I find inside.

Ariana is wrapped in a white bath towel and dancing around with her back to me. Her ass sways side to side as she moves to the beat of whatever music she's listening to on her AirPods. She twirls around and screams, startling backward, nearly losing her footing. One hand flies up to her chest, and the other tugs out one of her AirPods.

"Jesus, you scared the shit out of me."

"I thought something was wrong. I called you and knocked on the door several times."

Looking a little chagrined, she pulls out the other AirPod. "I wanted to have a shower after traveling." It's then she notices her state of undress, and she glances down at herself.

My dick really homes in on it too, because it jerks to life in my pants.

"Don't be long. It's no good if it's cold." I turn and leave the room, not bothering to close the door, but I hear it close behind me.

I take my plate, settle in on the end of the dining room table, and begin eating. A few minutes later, Ariana appears.

"You look different." The words slip from my mouth before I can think them through.

Her steps falter, but she keeps coming toward me. "Not sure how to take that." She picks up her plate and sits to the right of me.

I clear my throat. "I just mean that you look a lot younger like that." I gesture with my steak knife to her outfit and her hair.

The red locks are still wet, and she's pulled them into a messy bun at the top of her head. She doesn't normally wear a lot of makeup, but she's completely fresh-faced at the moment, and she has on a tank top and a pair of cotton shorts I think might actually be a pajama set.

It's all just a reminder of the deep chasm separating us—our ten-year age gap, the difference in our bank accounts, and her innocence compared to how soiled I am.

"Still not sure how to take it." She removes the silver dome and sets it to the side, looks at her plate, then over at me. "How did you know how I like my steak?"

Do I tell her that I asked Marcel to find out from the cook?

No.

"Lucky guess." I shrug and cut another piece of steak for myself.

She looks as though she doesn't know what to make of that and takes the first cut into her steak. I watch as she brings the fork to her lips and places the piece of meat between her plump lips, then I look away before I get any ideas.

When she's done swallowing, she says, "You know I could say the same thing about you."

My forehead creases. "What are you talking about?"

She looks me up and down. "I've never seen you dressed like that. It's weird."

I can't help but chuckle. "Weird?"

"You're always the portrait of a billionaire—in your bespoke suits, hair perfectly coiffed, put together in a way not many can manage."

I can't help but preen at her description of me. "So, which do you prefer?" There's a small amount of flirtation in my voice.

"I don't have a preference. You're my boss," she says as she cuts another piece of steak. But she won't look at me.

"Say it enough, and maybe you'll believe it."

Her head whips in my direction, and her eyes narrow the slightest amount. "Don't worry. I realize your T-shirt probably costs more than all the clothes I came to the manor with."

She might be correct, but I see her comment for what it is— a way to erect a wall between us.

If I were smart, I'd let her. But I still can't seem to help myself from wanting more from her. Always *more.*

CHAPTER
FOURTEEN

ARIANA

The thing I realize within five minutes of our first meeting is that the Obsidian Voss I know from Midnight Manor is not the same Obsidian Voss who shows up to meetings.

Here, he's the most charming man in the room and has everyone eating out of his hand. There's zero trace of the predator I've had glimpses of. It's not that he doesn't seem powerful or that he's a pushover. It's that he knows exactly how to make people feel comfortable in his presence—in order to manipulate them into getting what he wants, all while making them think it's their idea.

By the third meeting, I wonder why he's not the CEO of Voss Enterprises, but then it makes sense. He'd be chained to a desk if that were the case, and the best use of his talents is out in the field, being the face of Voss Enterprises.

Each of our meetings is a chance for him to advocate for something to regulators on behalf of Voss Enterprises. Forget a team of lobbyists, Obsidian Voss is a one-man wrecking ball, destroying any arguments the other side has almost immediately, whether it be through his charm or through his intimate knowledge of the law.

If he didn't irritate me so much with his snide remarks and his hot and cold temperament, I might find it impressive.

The official meeting has broken up, and Obsidian is doing what he does with a bunch of senators on one of the committees he spoke with today. I'm on the other side of the room, speaking to one of their aides.

Before we arrived at the first meeting today, Obsidian made it clear that my job is to be seen and not heard and to take notes. I was to agree with anything he said, and if he got stuck in a conversation with the same person for longer than five minutes before or after a meeting, I was to interrupt and feign that something urgent needed his attention. And if I see him fix his left cuff link, that's the signal that he wants to be pulled out of the conversation, regardless of how long he's been talking to the person.

If I'm off on my own, my instructions are to be polite, but a little aloof. According to him, people need to know that I'm loyal to the Vosses because everyone is always looking for an angle. He described DC as a shark tank with chum in the water—sometimes you're the shark, and other times you're the chum.

One of the senator's aides, Brandon, and I are chatting. He seems nice enough, I guess, but I'm only half paying attention because I'm watching Obsidian, making sure he doesn't give me the signal.

"Will you be attending the fundraiser tonight?" Brandon asks me.

I look away from my boss and at him. Brandon's attractive. Maybe a few years older than I am, with dark blond hair and hazel eyes.

"Assuming there hasn't been a change of plans I don't know about, yes." I give him a warm smile.

"Wonderful. I do hope you'll save a dance for me then." His eyes spark with interest.

I shift in my spot, unsure how to handle this. "I'm not sure whether Mr. Voss will need me at all, but I might be able to spare a dance. We'll see." There, that was noncommittal.

Brandon speaks directly into my right ear. "If things go how they usually do at these things, by ten o'clock, all the old guys will already be half drunk. When that happens, they stop talking about politics and policies and actually remember how to have a good time."

A little uncomfortable with how close he is to me, I lean back. "Thanks for the tip."

My gaze darts over to Obsidian, who I know is watching us, and he doesn't look happy. It reminds me of the night he saw me with my brother. With that thought comes the memory of what happened in his car, and I have to squeeze my thighs together. Jerk.

Obsidian plays with his left cuff link. Of course he does.

"I need to go remind Mr. Voss about something. It was great meeting you. Maybe I'll see you tonight." A quick glance at Obsidian tells me he's still watching from the corner of his eye.

Brandon holds my elbow. My instinct is to pull away from his touch, but I force myself not to if only for the small pleasure of knowing it will irritate Obsidian.

"Make sure to save me that dance, and if I'm lucky, maybe you'll have a drink with me afterward."

I smile. "We'll see."

Then I turn and make my way over to the group of men Obsidian is standing with. They all notice me approaching, and I'd have to be blind not to see the way they check me out as I come to stand beside Obsidian. It makes me want to gag—besides Obsidian, they're all probably at least thirty years my senior.

He seems to notice as well because he bristles, and his expression darkens.

"Gentlemen." I give them all a polite nod. "Mr. Voss, you have a phone call scheduled in ten minutes. I just wanted to remind you."

He looks at me. "Thank you, Miss Clarke." Then he returns his attention to the men he's been holding court with. "Duty calls. Guess I'll see most of you tonight."

They all give a round of goodbyes, telling him it was good to see him again.

"Consider what I said," Obsidian says before directing me out of the room ahead of him.

He doesn't say anything to me until we're seated in the vehicle, and he's heading back to the hotel so we can eat dinner and get ready for the ball.

"How did you enjoy yourself today, Ariana?"

The way he asks the questions feels like a piece of cheese in a mouse trap.

"It was fine. Interesting to see how things actually get done in Washington behind the scenes." I stare out the passenger window.

"Was there something specific you enjoyed most?"

I don't bother turning to look at him. "Why don't you just ask what you really want to ask?"

"Was that pissant of an aide hitting on you?" He wastes no time by continuing the game.

I roll my eyes and adjust my posture so I'm turned toward him. "What is it with you? No, he was not hitting on me." Not much anyway.

"You sure about that?"

"Yes, I'm sure."

"If I find out you're lying..."

I throw up my hands. "You'll what?"

We stop at a red light, and he uses the opportunity to look at me, his gaze intense. "You don't want to find out."

That makes me a little nervous. "Well, it's a good thing he wasn't hitting on me then, I guess."

The light turns green, and he speeds away from the inter-section.

I STUDY myself in the full-length mirror in the bedroom and can hardly believe it's my own reflection I'm looking at.

A professional hair and makeup artist came to the suite to help me get ready. According to Obsidian, that's how things work in their circles. My hair has been swept up in a loose, low bun except for two pieces that frame my face, and my makeup is heavier than normal but not too much. The pink on my lips matches my dress, and the cat eye she gave me makes me look sultry.

And the dress... wow. I thought it was too much when I tried it on at home, but Marcel assured me I would fit in with everyone here. I don't know though. There's more cleavage than I'm used to showing. It's bright pink silk and strapless with a dip in the center that reminds me a little of something you might find in the fifties, except that it hugs my curves past my waist, and there's a slit over my right leg.

An impatient knock sounds on the door, and I grab the evening bag off the dresser and stride over to the door. When I open it, Obsidian takes me in from head to toe. His gaze feels like he's brushing his knuckles down the valley of my breasts.

His eyes heat for a moment before he covers it up with indifference. "Ready?"

I hate that seeing him appreciate the way I look sends a flare of desire through my limbs. What is wrong with me that I'm still attracted to this man? Why do I yearn to please him?

"Yup, let's go." I walk past him toward the door of the suite. I turn to hold the door open for him, but he still stands at my bedroom door. His eyes are closed, and he's pinching the bridge of his nose. "Are you coming?"

His head snaps up, and he glares at me, then stalks toward me in his tuxedo. He looks like the epitome of a powerful, rich, hot as hell man, and I suddenly understand what people mean when they say the man wears the suit, the suit doesn't wear the man.

It's an effort to keep the lust warming my veins from showing on my face. Instead, I mask it with irritation. "You're the one who wanted to go, so let's go."

He comes to stand with me, too close, reaching over my head and holding the heavy door open for me, then gestures out into the hall. "Ladies first."

He's morphing into the charming version of Obsidian. Shaking my head, I step out into the hallway. This man, I swear.

A couple hours later, I stand at the edge of the dance floor with a glass of white wine in my hand, watching as Obsidian dances with some woman he was talking to earlier. She's clearly a fan.

When I went over to try to relieve him earlier after he'd been talking to her for longer than his prescribed five minutes, he ignored my invitation to get out of the conversation and continued speaking with her.

Whatever. He's on his own for the rest of the night.

Her head falls back in laughter at something he says, and my hand tightens around the glass.

So far, tonight has been a fancier version of all our meetings in DC. People make promises to each other in a "you scratch my back, I'll scratch yours" sort of way. There are lots of talks about investments, the economy, and the occasional moments of gossip.

If I thought I might enjoy tonight because I've never been to anything like this, I was wrong. Obsidian has entirely ignored me and that rubs on the old wound left after my mom's abandonment. Which is completely ridiculous being that I barely know the man.

"Good to see you again."

I turn to my left and see the aide I spoke with earlier today, Brandon.

"Hey, how are you enjoying yourself?" I sip from my wine.

He shrugs. "If you've been to one of these, then you've been to them all. But my evening would get better if you gave me that dance."

His eyes are glossy, as if he's had too much to drink.

I'm not sure if I should dance with him. Not sure if I'm allowed to. Obsidian didn't say whether I was actually able to enjoy myself this evening.

As soon as that thought registers, I snarl in my head. One glance at Obsidian makes my decision for me. The woman he's dancing with whispers something in his ear, and I watch as his hand slips lower on her back.

I smile at Brandon. "I'd love to. Just let me set my wine down."

He reaches for the glass in my hand. "I've got it." He takes it from me and walks over to a nearby table, setting it near the edge. He offers me his elbow. "Shall we?"

I slide my arm through his, and he leads me onto the dance floor.

"This probably isn't the best time to admit that I don't know what I'm doing out here. I'm only accustomed to the kind of slow dancing you do in high school."

Brandon chuckles and takes one hand, sliding his other one onto my back. "Follow my lead then."

"Promise I'll try not to step on your toes," I say.

I fumble for the first minute, then I get the hang of it. I won't be winning any dance competitions, but I'm not stepping on Brandon's toes or tripping over my own feet, so I count it as a win.

"How often do you think you'll be visiting DC now that you're working for Voss Enterprises?" he asks.

"I'm not really sure. I expect that Mr. Voss will have me in tow whenever he needs to be here. I'm new to the corporation, so I'm not sure how often that is."

Brandon smiles at me, gaze intent. "Probably at least once a month then. Maybe I can take you out next time you're in town. Dinner."

A feeling of discomfort tightens my chest, and I can't pinpoint why exactly. But I'm a single woman, free to do what I want when I'm not being paid by Voss Enterprises, so I push away my unease and nod. "That would be nice."

Triumph passes over Brandon's face, and he pulls me closer to him as the song ends. Another one starts up immediately. Brandon leans into me, but someone taps my shoulder, and I turn to see Obsidian waiting and glowering.

CHAPTER

FIFTEEN

"We need to talk," he barks. Then, seeming to remember that we're not alone, his public façade slides on, and he says, "Care to dance while we do it?" He looks over my shoulder and gives Brandon a smile.

I turn back to Brandon. "Sorry. I'll come find you after I take care of whatever he needs."

The hand on my back squeezes me. "Looking forward to it." Then Brandon nods at Obsidian and leaves the dance floor.

Obsidian's hand is on my upper arm, spinning me around to face him immediately, then he pulls me into his arms. He doesn't say anything as he spins me around the dance floor, and I'm loath to admit that he's much smoother than Brandon.

"I thought you needed to talk to me?" I ask after he hasn't spoken for a minute.

He doesn't respond, but he grips me closer.

The press of my body against his feels impossible to ignore. Every time we move, my breasts slide against his hard chest, and a few times when I misstep, our thighs brush. Slowly, his hand snakes farther down my back until it's resting just above my ass.

Is he trying to drive me mad?

"Obsidian, what did you need to talk to me about?"

He stops us from moving and pulls back enough to look at me. An unnamed emotion swirls in his eyes. "That's the first time you've said my name."

My cheeks heat. "I'm sorry, it was inappropriate. I'm just frustrated because you interrupted and said we needed to talk and then—"

"No, I want you to use it when no one else is around. No more Mr. Voss."

Our gazes lock until it feels too intimate, and I look away. I don't know what to say to that, especially because it feels like it means something. As though it's moved our relationship forward in a way I can't understand. And so, I say nothing, no longer bothering to ask what he wanted to talk to me about.

He spins me around the dance floor, holding me closer than is appropriate, and his breaths make the fine hairs that have escaped my bun ruffle against my bare neck. My eyes drift closed, and I imagine the heavier, deeper breaths he might exhale if he were over me, ruthlessly fucking me.

My nipples pebble beneath the silk of my dress, and I grow wet between my thighs. I've never felt like this around another man. It's not like I've never been turned on before, but I've never been turned on *just* by being around someone. Never imagined myself being with him just because he was near.

As if he can sense the change of my thoughts, Obsidian's hand clenches my lower back, pulling me closer to him. I don't dare turn my head to look at him because I know it would put our mouths millimeters apart, and I don't trust myself not to kiss him.

The more we dance, the more my yearning builds and builds. When the song finally ends, all I can think to do is run from it, from him.

I step back, looking at the floor. "I need to use the restroom."

Liar.

Turning, I dash off the dance floor, pushing a little impolitely through the mass of people. I need to remove myself from his orbit before I do something stupid. Something even more stupid than stealing from the man.

I turn to look over my shoulder to make sure he's not following, and as I'm turning back around, I run into someone.

"I'm so sorry," I rush out.

Large hands settle on my upper arms to keep me from stumbling back. "Where's the fire?" Brandon says with a smile.

My gaze dips down, not sure what excuse to give him for why I'm hurrying off the dance floor. But he doesn't make me give him one.

"Want to get some fresh air somewhere quieter?" he asks.

I nod. "Yes, yes, that would be great." Anything to get away from Obsidian and everything he makes me feel.

Brandon takes my hand and leads me through the crowd, out of the ballroom, and down the hall.

"Where are we going?" I ask, second-guessing my decision.

"Somewhere less crowded, like I said."

When I hear the ballroom door open behind me, I turn and look over my shoulder, panicking that maybe it could be Obsidian. But it's just a woman heading in the opposite direction down the hall toward the bathrooms.

We turn a corner and walk down another hall toward a wall of glass I realize leads to a balcony. Good, I need fresh air.

He opens the door, and I step outside, drawing in a deep breath in an effort to calm my mind and my libido.

Brandon comes up behind me and places his hands on my shoulders, squeezing. "You're tense."

"Long day," I say as an excuse. I'm about to ask him to remove his hands, but then he massages the muscles, and it feels so good the words die on my tongue.

"You look wonderful tonight," he says.

"Thank you." I wish his complimentary words made my heart pick up speed the way that just a look from Obsidian can.

"Is this helping?" he asks.

"Very much." My chin drops toward my chest, and I enjoy the tension leaving my muscles. When he removes his hands, I turn to face him. "Thank you. That feels much better."

"It's a grind working for these people, I know."

I give an exasperated sigh and shake my head. "I'm starting to see that."

"Maybe I can help take the edge off." He places his hands on either side of my face and brings his mouth to mine.

I'm so shocked that it takes me a moment to register what's happening. I mean, he seems like an okay guy and all, and we've enjoyed a nice conversation tonight, but what gave him the idea that I wanted to make out with him?

I turn my head to the side, but instead of taking it for the polite rejection it is, he kisses his way down my neck.

My hands move to his shoulders in an attempt to push him away. "Brandon, wait." When his tongue runs over my collarbone, I push harder. "Wait, stop."

He brings his mouth up to my ear. "It's okay. No one is going to catch us." He nibbles on my earlobe, and my eyes squeeze shut.

I attempt to pull away, but he holds me there with the hand on the other side of my head. "Please stop." I again try to push him away, but he won't budge.

"What did you think was going to happen when I led you away from the party?" His lips crash against mine.

I try to turn my face away from the kiss, but his hand grazes over my dress, clutching my breast, and I freeze. He takes that as acquiescence, and his touch gets rougher as he moves to kiss my neck again.

"No, stop!" I cry, beating on his shoulders with tears in my eyes.

"Stop pretending you don't enjoy this." He yanks down one side of my dress, revealing my breast, and gropes me.

Panic flares in my chest, and when he brings his mouth back to mine, I bite down hard on his bottom lip.

"Fuck!" He pulls away with his hand to his lip and looks at me with fury in his eyes.

Unlike when Obsidian has looked at me in anger, there's something different about this, and instinctively, I know this man will have no problem hurting me.

Before he can say or do anything, I bolt around Brandon and race through the door. I try to remember how we got here, tugging my dress up over my breast as I run as fast as I can in my heels while he calls my name from behind me.

I will the tears in my eyes not to fall, at least not until I'm alone. Somehow, I end up coming in on the opposite side of the ballroom than the one we left. As soon as I'm inside, I look frantically for Obsidian. I'm not sure why, but he feels like a safety net. All I want to do is leave this place.

It takes me a couple of minutes, but eventually I find Obsidian chatting with a group of men. I stop several feet away, unsure how to interrupt and unsure whether I can keep myself together enough not to let on how upset I am. But I don't have to figure it out because Obsidian must sense my presence. He takes one glance at me, and alarm flashes across his face before he schools his features and says something to the men to excuse himself, then prowls toward me.

He doesn't slow down as he takes my elbow as he passes, turning me around and leading me toward the exit. "What happened? What's wrong?" He nods politely at someone who says hello as we pass by.

I shake my head and sniffle, unable to push out the words.

He stops us outside the ballroom and studies me for a beat. "C'mon, we're leaving."

He leads us to the valet and hands him our ticket. We wait in silence while the valet retrieves our vehicle. Even though it's a warm summer evening, I shake—shock maybe? I wrap my arms around myself to try to keep it together. Warm fabric slides over my skin, and I find Obsidian wrapping his tuxedo jacket over my shoulders.

"Thank you." For some reason, that gesture of kindness makes me want to bawl. Instead, I wrap the jacket tighter around myself, inhaling deeply because it smells like him and that feels like comfort.

I nestle into the fabric warmed by his body heat, and by the time the valet brings the car to a stop in front of us, the shaking has subsided.

Obsidian waves off the valet and opens the passenger door for me, helping me in and closing the door before taking a seat behind the wheel. He looks at me with concern, then puts the car in drive and surges forward.

We don't speak on the ride back to the hotel, which I'm thankful for. I wouldn't know what to say. I think I'm still in shock at what happened.

I've been involved in a lot of shady shit in my life, but I've never felt threatened in that way until tonight. I can't help but think back over all my interactions with Brandon and wonder whether I did something to lead him on.

"We're here."

Obsidian's voice cuts through my thoughts, and I realize we've arrived at the hotel. He exits the driver's seat and comes over to my side, helps me out of the car, and leads me by the hand into the hotel.

He continues to hold my hand across the lobby, and I can't find it in me to pull away. It's not until we're inside the suite, and I hear the door click and lock, that I burst into a sob, unable to hold back the rising tide of emotions inside me.

"Hey, hey, hey." Obsidian wraps his arms around me and draws me into him. The scent of his cologne and the feel of his warm body is welcoming, and I nuzzle into his chest.

The tears come harder as he rubs my back. Somehow, him being so nice and gentle with me has me even more upset.

"Whatever it is, it's okay. We'll figure it out."

I shake my head against his chest, unable to stop the tears.

I'm lucky I got out of the situation when I did—otherwise, who knows what would have happened? It's relief, shock, and the reality that if Brandon had more time, there's likely not much I could have done to stop him that makes the tears keep coming.

My chest squeezes painfully, and it takes a moment for me to register that Obsidian has picked me up and is walking us over to the couch. He sits and settles me on his lap with one arm wrapped around my back.

He wipes the tears from my cheeks with his large fingers, gentler than I would have thought he could be. "Will you tell me what happened?"

Embarrassment makes my face flush. The idea of explaining it to him has me shaking my head.

His gaze roams my face, and there's no judgment, only genuine concern. "Are you sure? It might make you feel better. Maybe I can help."

My lips press together, and tears gather in my eyes again, but I do tell him. Because the truth is that this is the first time I've felt safe and protected in a long time. I love my father, but I never had that feeling growing up. He was always dragging us into trouble, not rescuing us from it.

By the time I'm done explaining what happened, Obsidian's face is a mask of cold fury, though I know instinctively it's not directed at me. He just stares at me, unblinking.

"Say something," I whisper.

He blinks, coming out of whatever trance he's in. "I'm resisting the urge to bolt from this room, track him down, and show him what it's like when someone puts their hands on you when you don't want them to." In juxtaposition to his words, he runs his knuckles lightly down my cheek.

A part of me would take great satisfaction in letting him do just that. But I don't want any more attention on what happened than what Obsidian's already giving me, so I shake my head.

"You can't do that. You'd get in trouble, and then everyone would know what happened." I turn my head to look away from him.

"Don't worry about me getting into trouble, Ariana." Obsidian gently uses his thumb and forefinger to turn my head back in his direction. "I'm not going to tell you how to feel about what happened, but you shouldn't feel shame. Do you want to report it to the authorities?"

I look at him, horrified. "Absolutely not. It would just be my word against his. And I don't know... maybe it's partly my fau—"

"Don't you dare finish that sentence," he growls. "That's bullshit. I don't care how tempting you look tonight, how much you smiled at him, or how good the conversation was. The minute you told him to back off, he should have. End of. Don't you dare take on any responsibility because he felt entitled to help himself to something that wasn't his to take. Understand?"

"Okay, I know you're right, it's just..."

"I get it. But you did nothing wrong, okay?" He tilts his head so our eyes meet.

"Okay."

The tension in his body dissipates. "Why don't you go take your makeup off and get changed? Have a shower if you like."

The idea of a shower sounds divine. "Good idea."

He helps me off his lap, and I stand awkwardly.

"Thanks for…" I want to say thanks for being so gentle and kind and sweet, but I stop myself. "Getting me out of there so quickly."

He shoves his hands in his pockets. "Of course."

I turn to walk away.

"Ariana," he calls, and I circle back around. "If you want to talk to someone, a professional, about what happened, I can arrange that."

"Have a therapist on speed dial, do you?" I smirk, knowing there's no chance this man is regularly baring his soul on some doctor's couch.

"What do you think?" he says wryly. "No, but I can make it happen if you think it would help you."

I give him a small smile. "I appreciate the offer, and I'll let you know."

He nods reluctantly, and I continue to my bedroom.

After a long hot shower, I emerge from the bedroom back into the main part of the suite. I asked Marcel to get me some proper pajamas before the trip so that I wouldn't be sleeping in a T-shirt and panties like the time I ran into Obsidian in the garden.

A movie is cued up on the TV, and on the coffee table in front of the couch is a tray of delicious looking apple crullers.

"Where did these come from?" I sit on the couch, looking at Obsidian where he sits in the chair off to the side.

"I made a call while you were showering." He shrugs as if it's no big deal.

"But how did you know I wanted to try these?" I pick up one and take a big bite, moaning when the sweetness hits my tongue.

"You think I didn't notice the way you looked longingly at them in that bakery when we grabbed a coffee the past two days?" A small smile tilts the corner of his lips.

He's not wrong. I have been eyeballing them each time we've grabbed a coffee at the bakery near where all our meetings have been. I just didn't want sticky hands and the sugar crash, which is why I refrained from ever grabbing one. But the fact that he was paying attention makes my chest squeeze.

"Well, thank you." I take another bite, not sure what his nice act says and not wanting to read any more into his small act of kindness.

He reaches for the remote off the coffee table and hits a button that starts the movie on the TV.

"Didn't figure you for a rom-com guy." In fact, the idea feels ridiculous.

"Figured you might enjoy something light and entertaining."

Our gazes hold, and I nod in thanks, then turn my attention to the TV, wishing that Obsidian's reaction to the awful thing that happened tonight didn't make me want him more.

CHAPTER

SIXTEEN

OBSIDIAN

When I wake the next day, the urge to fly out of bed and track down that little prick Brandon still presses against my sternum. I don't because I don't want to leave Ariana alone and because I want to give her the space to decide how she wants to deal with it.

That doesn't mean I won't take my revenge on him if Ariana doesn't take hers, but the wound is still fresh, and she may not really know what she wants to do at this point.

I understand the impetus to want to forget it. My mother did the same thing for many years with my father. Hell, I did the same thing for years with my father.

What it comes down to is that I'll give her whatever she needs—time, space, more apple crullers, it doesn't matter.

Because seeing her broken last night triggered something I can't seem to unravel.

I've been committed to trying to get rid of her, and now all I want is to pull her closer and tuck her into my side, protecting her from any harm. I don't even know what the fuck that means. Sure, I want to bed her, but this urge, this is more than just my dick talking.

We're leaving shortly to head back to Midnight Manor, and I'm all packed up, waiting in the living area of the suite, but Ariana hasn't made an appearance yet.

Is she okay? Should I go check on her?

Jesus, these thoughts are going to drive me fucking nuts. Before last night, I would've just barged into her room and told her to get her ass moving. It was all much simpler before she worked her way under my skin and burrowed in so deep I can't get her out.

I'm saved from having to ponder what to do further when her bedroom door opens and she strolls out, wheeling her suitcase behind her. She's dressed in a slim fitted pair of beige dress pants and black lace blouse with short sleeves. Her eyes aren't puffy, so I don't think she's been crying this morning, which eases the tightness in my chest.

"How are you feeling this morning?" I ask, walking toward her and holding out my hand for her suitcase.

She seems surprised, but she passes it over. "I'm okay. Still a little shaken, but better than last night, thanks." Her big blue eyes look up at mine.

I've grown accustomed to seeing disdain in them, irritation, and the occasional flare of lust, but this morning, there's something new there—a wary sort of adoration. The way that makes my throat burn, how it makes me wish, makes me hope, I could be someone different than I am so I could be worthy of that look... my jaw tics.

Hope.

Hope is such a vicious, insidious thing.

How many times did I have faith and hope that my mother would leave my father? That my father would change, morph into something he wasn't? And then, as I grew older and realized that would never happen, all I'd hope for was that he'd die and we'd never have to bear the brunt of him again. And then he did, and it didn't change anything—his torture remained even after he was buried in the earth. It was just a different kind of torture.

Hope has never done anything for me except disappoint me.

"Obsidian?"

Ariana's voice draws me from my thoughts, and I realize she said something to me. "Sorry?"

"I just thanked you again for being so great yesterday." Her eyes shine at me like two pools of deep blue water, expectant. Probably for me to continue being the guy I was last night.

But I can't do that. I can't let her hope like I once did, only for it to destroy her in the end.

So rather than tell her I'd have it no other way, that I want to do whatever I can to ease her pain, I just give her a gruff grunt and bite out, "Let's go. We're already running late because of you."

A flash of hurt lands on her face, then something like steely determination creeps over her features. Without a word, she strides toward the door and holds it open while I carry our suitcases through.

"I can take mine," she says as we walk toward the elevator.

"I've got it."

We don't speak as we make our way down to the lobby, wait for the valet to bring around the car, or on the ride to the private airport. Which should be fine. Should be what I want. But instead, it's eating at me because I want to hear her lyrical voice.

Finally, when we get on the plane, she takes her seat across from me and checks her company phone, then looks at me. "Your three thirty had to cancel, so I've moved up your five o'clock call so that you can be done early if you want."

It feels like a small balm to my soul, as inane as the words are.

But I still can't cave to the look in her eyes. The one that says she wants to go back to last night's Obsidian. So I simply close my eyes and feign sleep for most of the flight.

HOURS LATER, we land at the private airport closest to Midnight Manor, and it's clear to me that something shifted in Ariana's demeanor while we were airborne. I can't describe it exactly, but she's carrying herself differently.

I suppose it should be no great surprise when we take a seat in my vehicle to drive home, and she immediately turns to me.

"I know what you're doing."

I ignore her, pulling out of the airport and onto the road.

"You're pushing me away. We've both been ignoring whatever this is between us, whatever this pull is, but I think we should talk about it."

Glancing over quickly, I see that she's turned in her seat and is facing me, studying me.

"Last night, something terrible happened, and you were there for me. We connected in a way we haven't before, something that felt like more than just a physical attraction, and now you're running scared."

I swallow hard, and my hands tighten on the steering wheel. Am I that transparent? "I'm not running scared of anything."

"I think you are. And I don't think it's the first time you've done so with me. Last night proved it."

I shake my head. "You're young, Ariana. You're making things up in your head, romanticizing things. There is nothing between us." I signal and make a right off of the main road.

"So, finger fucking me the night you were jealous over my brother was nothing?"

"A temporary lapse of judgment." My dick twitches from the words coming off her tongue and the memory of her hand down her panties.

"I don't believe you." She leans over the console and runs her tongue along the side of my neck, over the wolf tattoo. "You have no idea how long I've wanted to do that," she whispers in my ear.

My eyes drift closed for a beat, and my hands tighten on the steering wheel. Her tongue felt like warm silk sliding over my skin.

"Get back in your seat," I snap, but there's no bite to my words.

"Make me," she says, sliding her hand down my chest, my waist, until her palm settles over my now half-hard cock.

I bite back a groan as she rubs my cock. I'm a bastard because I don't immediately stop her. I wait for ten, twenty, thirty seconds until I'm fully hard and pressing against the seam of my pants.

"You don't want to do this."

"I do." Her tongue flicks my earlobe.

My foot presses down harder on the gas pedal, and the car launches forward, her teeth anchoring to my earlobe.

"I am not the man you think I am."

Her fingers manipulate my belt, then the button of my slacks. "You say that, yet I'm not sure that's true. You've put your worst foot forward with me. I don't know why, I don't understand it. But last night you showed me there's more to you. If last night taught me anything, it's that sometimes the person who presents themselves as the good guy is actually the opposite, and vice versa." She slides the zipper of my pants down and over, careful of the hardness that lies underneath.

"I'm not a good guy, Ariana." I chance a glance down at my lap as she coaxes my length out through the gap in my boxer briefs. Her delicate hand looks so tiny compared to my straining cock.

"Maybe. But I don't think you're an entirely bad one either."

She strokes my cock up and down. It takes everything in me to say my next words and not give into temptation.

"Your head is probably a mess. I don't want to take advantage of you." I might be a lot of things, but I could never live with myself if she woke up tomorrow and regretted anything.

She nuzzles her face into my neck as I take another turn, going too fast around the corner and sending her weight into me. "You're not, I swear. I just... I want to be in control. I want to take what I want... if you want to give it to me."

My chest cracks open because I understand that desire better than she could ever realize.

Ariana swirls her thumb around the precum leaking from the tip of my erection, and my foot slams on the accelerator.

"I don't want you to regret this."

As she brings her face down to my lap, her blue eyes rise to mine. "I would never regret this, Obsidian."

Then she wraps her lips around the head of my cock, and I'm helpless. The word no is no longer in my vocabulary.

She sucks on the end and swirls her tongue before sliding down and putting as much of me in her mouth as possible. A deep groan works its way from my chest as her fist strokes the bottom half of my dick.

"Christ, you're such a good fucking girl." I look away from the road for a second so that I can bear witness to what's happening and commit it to memory for eternity. "Perfection."

I return my eyes to the road if only so we won't crash, and this will continue. We're flying down the road, but it only adds to the sensation of what's happening below my waist.

Ariana continues to stroke me and suck me, and she gags a little when she goes even farther down my shaft. Fuck, her throat constricts around the end of my cock.

She works me so well that it seems like no time has passed before my balls draw up, ready to feed my cum into her mouth. She increases her pace, dragging me in and out of her mouth, and I can't help but increase the speed of the car in tandem.

Our gazes meet when I risk a quick look down at my lap, and it's obvious how much she's enjoying making me a slave to her ministrations. She squeezes tighter around my base, working me hard, and I hate that I have to return my eyes to the road.

One hand delves into her hair while the other squeezes the steering wheel. I try to hold out a little longer, but between the speed of the car and the way she's working me, it's a pointless endeavor.

I press harder on the gas and bite out a curse, my ass rising off the seat, coming in her mouth while she continues to pump me with her fist. She milks every drop out of me, and I take my foot off the accelerator and pull off onto the dirt shoulder. She pulls away from my lap and lifts her head, meeting my eyes.

The urge to kiss her is so strong. She stays in place, almost as though she's waiting for me to make the next move... but I can't. It's too intimate, and it's a bridge I can't cross. One I'm not sure I'll ever be able to.

So rather than leaning in and meeting her mouth with mine, I open my mouth and say, "We should get going. I have a call to make as soon as I return to my office."

Her disappointment is instantaneous. Her face falls, and she slides back over to her side, putting on her seat belt as I press the gas and turn back onto the road.

We don't speak for the rest of the day unless it's completely necessary, and even then, it's only work related. I suspect I've erected a permanent wall between us, which should fill me with relief.

So why does my chest ache if I'm getting exactly what I wanted?

CHAPTER

SEVENTEEN

Obsidian is back to being his cold self. If I'd hoped that what happened in his car would change things, I was sorely mistaken. If anything, it's only made him double down on presenting himself as an asshole.

I didn't see him at all yesterday since it was Saturday. And today, being Sunday, is dragging on. I'm anxious for the minutes to tick by and reach Monday morning, when I'll be back in Obsidian's orbit, even if he will do his best to ignore me.

Per usual, I met my brother at Black Magic Bar yesterday to pass off a set of silver candlesticks. With every week that goes by, I feel guiltier and guiltier about what I'm doing.

After everything that went down this week, guilt whirls around me like a tornado, seeping in through my pores. But then Bastion will tell me what he fetched for the previous week's steal, and I'll justify what I'm doing as necessary to save the people I love, as well as myself.

But after seeing that side of Obsidian after what Brandon did, I almost couldn't bring myself to put the candlesticks in my bag before I left the manor last night.

I don't regret what happened in the car on the way home from the airport, even if it didn't result in Obsidian taking me to bed once we arrived at Midnight Manor. I needed to feel in control, like I told him. And I didn't want to put off my next sexual encounter with a man—for fear that my feelings about what Brandon did would fester inside me and I would find it too hard. I needed to get it out of the way and prove to myself that I could still be turned on, still see sex as something enjoyable.

What Brandon did still lurks in the back of my mind, like a warning about what some men are capable of. It's not a lesson I'll soon forget, but I don't want to dwell on it. Don't want to give him the power to affect my life in that way.

It's hot out today, so I slip on my bikini to spend some time swimming and lounging by the pool. It has a purple triangle top with a teal green bottom, and I slide on the white oversized button-up I use as my cover-up, then leave my room. I'm sure to bring a bag with sunscreen, my phone and AirPods so I can listen to music, as well as a book.

It might be the height of summer outside, but the manor still feels dim inside, the bright sunshine not permeating past the heavy curtains or the thick glass in the Gothic windows. Everything here is more subdued. A prickle of awareness makes the hair stand up on the back of my neck —that has happened a few times since I arrived here.

It brings to mind the early morning I found Obsidian in the secret garden and the trail of sand that led me there. I'd forgotten about it with everything going on, but now I question whether I dreamed it or was sleepwalking or something. It feels so far from reality and everything that has happened since.

My skin heats as soon as I step into the sunshine. I slip my sunglasses from the top of my head over my eyes and walk across the patio over to one of the plush chaise loungers, then set my bag and cover-up on the table.

After I've applied my sunscreen, I decide to relax in the sun before I take a dip in the crystal-blue water. I'm not sure I've ever seen the weather so nice since I started staying here. It's as if a permanent cluster of clouds drapes itself over the manor. In the morning, tendrils of fog often dot the grounds. I want to enjoy the sun and water while I can.

My eyes drift closed behind my sunglasses, and I'm halfway to sleep when a throat clears next to me. My eyes snap open.

Marcel stands off to the side, hands behind his back. "I saw you out here. Wanted to see if you'd like a refreshment."

"That's so nice of you. Would you happen to have any lemonade?"

He nods. "Of course. I'll be right back."

"Thanks, Marcel."

Now that I'm no longer half asleep, I realize how warm my skin is, and I decide to get into the water to cool off. I set my sunglasses on the table and step over to the edge of the pool.

Ever since I was little, I've loved the water. Didn't matter if it was a pool, a lake, or the ocean. Even a river or a stream could keep me mildly content. My dad moved us around a lot, but I was always happiest when we lived near the water.

I dive in and tread water for a bit, enjoying the feel of the sun warming the top of my head. Then I lie on my back in the water and float with my eyes closed.

Growing bored, I decide to test myself to see if I can swim from one end of the oversized pool to the other without coming up for air. It's a game Bastion and I used to play as kids. I swim over to the shallow end to start and count myself down from three in my head, then push off the wall.

I swim with all my might, eyes open under the water. When I approach the edge of the deep end, a shadow casts down in the pool.

Marcel must have returned with my lemonade.

I'm running out of breath, but I push myself and touch the wall, coming up out of the water sucking in a big breath, ready to thank Marcel for the drink once I have enough oxygen, but it's not Marcel. It's Obsidian.

"Oh." I let go of the wall, treading water. "I thought you were Marcel."

He frowns. "Why would you think that?"

"He's getting me a drink." Using both hands, I push up out of the pool as gracefully as I can.

Obsidian doesn't step back to give me any extra room once I'm out. His gaze floats down my body, and I'm very aware that I'm practically naked in front of him. Sure, it's a swimsuit, but he's never seen me such minimal clothing.

My nipples pebble despite the stifling heat, and when his gaze tracks back up my body, it stops at my breasts. His nostrils flare and his hands twitch as though he wants to touch them.

"Is there a work emergency?" It's all I can think to ask because why else would he be here? He very clearly regrets what happened in his car—both times. Which is funny since he was worried I would regret it.

"No, there's no emergency."

"What are you doing here then?"

He pushes his hand through his hair. "Can you put on a cover-up or something? You make it hard to think."

My lips tilt into a smile. "Sure."

I walk past him and know that he's checking out my ass, so I add a little extra swagger to my hips. He may not want to want me, but he does. I can't help the way I want to preen at the knowledge, even knowing that I'm making an impossible situation even more impossible. If Obsidian ever knew who I really was, why I was really here... he'd treat me like he is now.

Making a show, I bend over and slide my sunglasses onto the top of my head, holding my wet hair back, then grab my cover-up. Straightening, I slide my arms into it and turn around, not bothering to button it.

I'm enjoying this game of cat and mouse. Today I'm the mouse, and I can't help hoping that he'll reach out and swat me.

His jaw hardens when I turn around without the shirt buttoned. "I want to show you something."

My head tilts. "I thought you said there wasn't anything pressing for work?"

He lets out a long sigh as though I'm the one exasperating *him*. "Just come on."

I slide on my sandals while he strides back to the double doors leading into the house. Marcel comes through before we make it there, my drink in hand.

I rush around Obsidian and take the drink from him. "Thank you so much, Marcel."

He nods. "Sir, can I get you anything?"

Obsidian shakes his head. "No, I'm fine, Marcel, thanks."

I take a big sip of the sweet and tart liquid before I follow bossy pants again. I'm not entirely sure where we're going, but when we pass the stained-glass wolf, I know it's in his wing of the manor.

He leads me to the very end of the hallway where there's a wooden door and pulls a skeleton key from the pocket of his pants. It might be Sunday, but Obsidian is dressed impeccably as always. He's wearing a pair of expensive beige chinos and a knit navy short-sleeve shirt with the two buttons on the V open. The universe could pluck him from here and set him in the center of the Amalfi Coast or Monaco, and he would fit right in.

He swings open the door and gestures for me to go ahead. When I walk through, I stop, surprised to see a set of stairs. Stairs that turn in a spiral. We must be entering the turret at the end of the east wing.

I look over my shoulder at him, feeling a little unsure, and he looks at me expectantly as impatience tightens his features. I don't know what this is, but I want to find out, whatever it is. If only because it means I'll get to spend more time in Obsidian's presence.

God, I am so messed up. That's the last thing I should want.

I walk up the steps, and it takes a couple minutes to reach the top. There's a landing and another closed door. Obsidian walks around me and produces the key again, unlocking the door. He opens it, and this time, he steps inside first and waits for me to join him.

My eyes are wide as I enter the large, circular room. Inside are tables and rows of custom shelves curved perfectly to sit flush against the walls. And on the tables and the shelves are all kinds of... artifacts? A collection of sorts.

I step farther inside, circling around in wonder. "What is this place?"

"They're things I've collected in my travels."

When I step to the table closest to me, there are some old maps partially unrolled, a purple crystal, and a gold fork. When I pick it up, I realize it must be solid gold because it's heavy.

"That's from a shipwreck that was discovered in the Caribbean."

I set it down and look around the room again. "You've traveled to a lot of places."

He steps closer to me. "I have to travel quite a bit for Voss Enterprises. And there was a period of time in my early twenties where I traveled extensively. Any time I didn't have to be in school, I headed off somewhere."

There's something almost melancholic about the expression on his face. "You didn't come back here?"

"No."

He offers no further explanation, so I drop it and move to the next table.

We go on like that for some time—I show interest in something, and he explains its origin, why it's meaningful to him. I'm not sure why he's brought me here, but I savor every word out of his lips because it feels as if he's revealing another hidden part of himself to me.

Finally, after half an hour or so passes, I turn to him. "Why did you decide to start collecting these things?"

He shrugs. "I'm not even really sure. It started when I was a boy." He looks out through the French doors that lead to a balcony. "I think maybe it started because I wanted to remember other places I'd been. Places better than this one."

I can't help it. I place a hand on his chest and pain flickers in his eyes. He looks down and meets my gaze with his twin pools of black.

"Why did you want to show me all of this?" I ask quietly.

He fingers a piece of damp hair hanging over my shoulder. "It's my way of apologizing for how I acted after what happened on the way back from the airport. That, and I saw the way you're always studying the relics throughout the manor whenever we're making our way from one room to another. I thought you might enjoy it."

Guilt shoves its way down my gullet, pushing down all the affection that was there moments ago. The only reason I'm doing that is so I know what to steal.

I clear my throat and step back. "I appreciate it." I turn and grab the first thing I see on a nearby shelf. "What's the significance of this one?"

He frowns. "It's sand from the beach of the last vacation we took as a family before my mom was murdered."

I blink at him in shock.

"It was an amazing getaway because my father didn't come." He tucks his hands in his pockets, almost as though he doesn't know what to do with them.

"Obsidian, your mom was murdered?" I place the sand-filled glass container on the shelf and walk over to him, my chest tight. I didn't see anything about that when I was researching him, but I guess I was looking at more recent articles, not delving into his past that far back.

He looks down at the floor.

"That's awful." My hand goes to his hard chest again, and the comfort I feel at the heat of his skin through the thin fabric should concern me.

"It was. I was eight when it happened."

"What happened? I mean, you don't have to talk about it if you don't want to." I search his face.

His large hand comes to my face, and he palms my cheek. "Why does it feel like I can tell you anything, Ariana? Why are you so different from anyone who's come before you?"

"I could ask you the same thing," I whisper.

EIGHTEEN

There's something akin to wonder in his dark eyes. When he doesn't say anything for a beat, I tell him again. "You don't have to tell me the details. I know what it's like to not have your mother in your life."

His gaze intensifies. "Your mother died too?"

I shake my head. "No. Actually, I don't know. Maybe. She took off when I was five. I haven't seen or heard from her since then." The familiar ache in my chest that's always there when I speak about my mom returns.

A crease deepens between his brows. "My mom had a long-term affair with one of my dad's rivals, and he stabbed her in the heart with a pair of garden shears when she finally told him she wouldn't leave my dad for him."

My eyes widen as realization dawns, remembering him early that morning and the way he looked so forlorn when he looked past me at the garden. "In the secret garden?"

He nods, and the air rushes from my lungs.

I cup his face, and he leans into my touch. "I'm so sorry. I can't imagine, especially since you were just a child."

He squeezes his eyes shut, and the pain on his face makes me want to wrap this man in my arms and take care of him. So I do.

I wrap my arms around his waist, hugging him and bringing my cheek to his chest. His heart beats strong and steady, reminding me of the kind of man he truly is. That night after Brandon assaulted me and right now—in pain or not—Obsidian is always a strong and steady force.

Maybe that's why I'm drawn to him. I'd do anything for my father and brother, but very few times have I ever felt I could really rely on them, that they wouldn't let me down in some way.

Obsidian stiffens in my arms, but slowly, he wraps his arms around me, then he rests his cheek against the top of my head.

My heart rate picks up at the nearness of him. We may have already traded orgasms, but this is different. This is more intimate than either of those events. This is something more than sexual gratification.

"What's going on between us, Obsidian?" The words burst from my lips before I can ponder whether they're wise to speak aloud.

To my surprise, he doesn't stiffen in my hold. He pulls back and looks at me, one hand resting where my neck meets my shoulder, his thumb lightly grazing up the column of my throat.

"I wish I knew. I can't seem to stop thinking about you. Stop wanting to be near you." He appears almost pained by his admittance.

"I feel the same. But I'm not sure it's wise." I'm a liar. I *know* it's not wise.

His gaze drops to my lips. "It's definitely not wise."

"But we're going to do it anyway, aren't we?" I whisper the truth that lies between us because this pull toward each other is too great to ignore.

He swallows and presses his lips together. "It can only be sex. I can't offer you anything more than that, even if I wish I could."

I'd be an even bigger liar if I tried to pretend his words don't lash me like a whip. But it's for the best, given that he doesn't know my true intentions.

"I'm fucked up, Ariana. In ways you can't even imagine." He's apologetic.

I nod. "I understand."

If we keep things strictly sexual, then it will be easier for me to leave, easier for me to continue lying to him than if feelings were involved.

"Do you, though?" He looks at me imploringly.

"I do." I raise up on my tiptoes to bring my lips to his, but he rears back.

"No kissing. It's too..."

He doesn't finish the sentence, but I know what he wants to

say. It's too intimate, too much like a relationship, too easy to forget that this is just about sex.

Though the disappointment stings, I nod. He waits a beat, seems to resolve something inside himself, and his eyes go from apprehensive and unsure to predatory and intense. I squeeze my thighs together because to be the object of that gaze is a heady thing indeed.

Without warning, he bends at his waist and lifts me over his shoulder. I yelp in surprise but love the caveman behavior and the display of his strength. He walks us across the room, opens one of the French doors to take us out to the balcony, and deposits me on...

"Holy shit." Once I get my bearings, I realize that he's sat me on the edge of the ledge. We're at least three stories up.

I clutch at his shirt in fear, but he's holding me by my ribcage so I won't fall. Still, one slip or wrong move, and I'm propelling to the ground.

"Obsidian—"

"Do you trust me?"

I meet his gaze, and it's obvious that my answer means something to him. My brain quickly cycles through what I know about him, how he reacted after the Brandon incident, the look on his face when he told me his mother had been murdered.

"I do." I relax under his hands.

Pure male satisfaction shines in his eyes. Like an animal pouncing on its prey, his mouth comes to the shell of my ear, his tongue darting out, and I can't help but wonder what it would feel like if he did that same thing to my clit.

He may not want to kiss my mouth, but he's definitely comfortable kissing down my neck until he reaches my breasts. "Pull your swimsuit aside."

I do as he says so that his hands remain on me, making sure I don't fall backward.

Obsidian's lips wrap around my puckered pink nipple, and I moan, lust firing to life in my veins. One hand goes into his hair, and the other delves down between us to feel his hard length pressing against his pants.

When I squeeze him, he groans and gently bites my nipple until I arch my head back. My sunglasses slide off my head. I turn to watch them spiral down, down, down to the ground. It's a reminder of how dangerous what we're doing is. Somehow, it's not a deterrent, only a turn-on.

My desire grows to a near frantic level where I'm desperate to have Obsidian.

He must feel it too, because he says, "Take me out, Ariana. I need to be inside you."

I do as he says, fumbling with the button and zipper on his pants until finally the length of him is in my palm. I stroke him. He pushes his hips forward, groaning around the weight of my breast.

"Obsidian..."

The word isn't a command, but the desperation in my voice is clear because he shifts to wrap one hand around my back while he slides his other hand between us, moving my swimsuit aside. Then he's pushing into me with one rough shove, filling me completely.

"I can't be gentle. I need you too much," he murmurs against the crook of my neck.

"I don't want you to be." I want everything this man has to offer. I want to bear witness to how wild I make him. He doesn't have to restrain himself with me.

With my reassurance, he pumps into me hard and fast. My arms wrap around him, sliding up under his shirt to feel the skin of his back. I slide them up and notice that the skin isn't smooth as it should be.

The thought flickers to darkness when Obsidian changes the angle of his hips, and we both cry out at the intensity of his thrusts. He stretches his neck and angles his face toward the sky, groaning. When the tattoo on his neck is stretched out, I realize it looks like a wolf howling at the moon.

He drops his head back down to look at me as he continues to piston inside me. "So good, Ariana. This. Is. So. Fucking. Good." He punctuates each word by slamming back inside me.

My orgasm builds until I'm frantic and desperate. My nails dig into the skin on his back as my orgasm bolts like an asteroid through the sky, red hot and unstoppable.

"Fuck yes, Ariana. Give it to me. Come all over my cock like a good girl."

He bites down where my neck meets my shoulder, and my climax hits me. I come harder than I ever have in my life. I cry out his name as my body splinters apart in ecstasy. The orgasm rolls through me again and again like waves crashing against the shore.

"That's it." There's pride in his tone.

His hands grip me tighter, his fingertips pressing into my skin hard enough to leave bruises. With a feral sound, he holds himself still and spills inside me. Every jerk of his cock is a victory as he continues until he's emptied himself.

We remain in that position, catching our breath, wrapped up in each other's arms for some time, the reality of what just happened settling in. I don't regret it, even if I have to push to the back of my mind the part of me that wants more than just this. It's not possible.

Once I've gained my bearings, I pull back. His wolf tattoo comes into view. I lean in once again and run my tongue over it. He hums in approval.

"Why did you decide to get the tattoo on your neck of all places? You're always so put together and charming in front of other people. This feels like it would give the opposite impression."

He pulls back enough to look in my eyes. "It's a reminder."

My head tilts. "Of what?"

"Of who I really am. Of what lurks under the surface."

My shoulders sink. I hate how he sees himself.

Before I can tell him, he pulls his softening cock from my body. The mixture of both our pleasure spills down the insides of my thighs.

Obsidian groans and pushes his hand through his hair, transfixed on the sight before he tucks himself into his pants. I hop off the ledge and right my bikini, though it doesn't do much in the way of making me presentable with his release running down my legs. I decide to do up the buttons on my cover-up.

"We didn't use protection."

My head snaps up from where I'm looking at my shirt. I'm on the pill, but still, what was I thinking? What was he thinking? He's a billionaire, and I can't think that women haven't tried to trap him into an unwanted pregnancy before.

"I'm on the pill," I say quickly in case he thinks that's what this was about. "And I haven't been with anyone since my last STI test."

He nods. "I'm in the clear for STIs, too."

"Okay, good." I give him a reassuring smile. "Probably something we should have discussed before we did that."

He draws me into his chest. "You're just too hard to resist. Especially in this bikini." He growls and nuzzles his face into my neck.

Today has been revealing in more ways than one. First, Obsidian showed me his treasure trove. Second, I now know what it's like to sleep with this man—life-changing. And there's one more thing I've figured out about him.

Obsidian Voss likes danger. He's an adrenaline junkie, at least when it comes to sex. He likes it to be dangerous. He wants to put him and his partner in positions that risk their lives and see how it turns out. The question is—why?

CHAPTER

NINETEEN

I thought I could fuck Ariana out of my system, but I was wrong. So fucking wrong.

Now that I know it's pure heaven to be balls deep inside her, I want her more than ever. It's a thirst that can never be quenched, an itch that can never be scratched.

Worse than that, she brings all my deepest desires to the surface. The desires I try to keep locked in a chest at the bottom of the ocean.

I think back to that day on the West Coast when I waded out into the ocean in the middle of a storm. Disappointment greeted me when I woke up on that beach, gasping for breath, but if I had never been saved, then I wouldn't have met Ariana, and somehow that feels like the real tragedy. Even more than if I had lost my life.

After we parted ways yesterday, Ariana went to take a shower, and I went to ponder my life choices, so I headed to the secret garden, wondering what I'd just done. The emotions Ariana stirs up inside me are like a funnel cloud, the desires... should I confess some part of them to her?

I push a hand through my hair and flop onto the couch in my office. I know myself. This need I have isn't going to go away on its own. I need to satisfy it somehow. The question is will Ariana let me, or will she run scared?

Her heels click on the floor as she enters the office then quiet when she steps onto the area rug. She pulls up short when she sees me sitting on the couch and not behind my desk.

She has on a pair of black dress shorts with a matching black belt and a green blouse tucked in. Christ, this woman's legs are what dreams are made of. I want them wrapped around my waist, thrown over my shoulders. I want to lick my way from her ankle to her inner thighs. I want—

"What's going on?"

Her melodic voice draws me from my musings.

"Why do you think something is going on?"

She walks over to where I am and sits on the couch, leaving a foot or so of space between us. "You never beat me here. And you're sitting on the couch, not behind your desk." Alarm flashes across her face, and she stiffens. "Don't tell me you're going hot and cold on me again and have changed your mind about our arrangement?"

A part of me, a big part, likes that she's worried I want to call it all off. But how will she feel when she realizes I want to up the ante, and what that involves?

I shake my head. "That's not what this is about."

Tell her. Tell her. Tell her.

Nerves make my chest tight, my breathing struggles. It's not as though I've never discussed my kinks with a sexual partner before, but it didn't matter what they thought of me. What they said and whether they agreed or not.

That's not true of Ariana. I wasn't lying when I said she's different from everyone who came before her.

"Obsidian, you're making me nervous. What's going on?"

My eyes drift closed for a beat when she says my name. It does something to me. Not many people use my given name, and the fact that she's gone from thinking of me as Mr. Voss to Obsidian feels like a victory.

"I need to talk to you about something, and I don't know how you're going to feel about it." I take her hand, needing her to ground me.

"That doesn't really help with the fact that you're making me nervous." Her beautiful blue eyes are wide and fixed on me.

I swallow hard. "Have you heard of somnophilia?"

She slowly shakes her head, obviously having no idea where I'm going with this conversation.

"I told you I'm messed up. One of the ways I'm messed up is with some sexual kinks that people might find... deviant."

Ariana tenses but waits patiently for me to continue.

There's no getting around it now. I might as well just come

out and say it. "It means engaging in sexual activity with a sleeping or unconscious person."

Her eyes flare open, and she rears back.

"I'm not into the unconscious thing. I don't want to drug you and have you knocked out. I want to sneak into your room at night and fuck you while you're sleeping. I want to take you when you're at your most vulnerable."

The words hang between us. She looks as if she's not sure how to respond, but I force myself not to fill the silence. I don't want to talk her into it or have to convince her. If she says yes, I want it to be because she wants to experiment with her sexuality, not because she's pleasing me.

"Won't I... wake up?" She bites her plump bottom lip.

I nod. "Of course. And that's fine. That's part of it for me."

She leans back into the couch cushion, looking down at her lap for a few moments.

I hold my breath, waiting for her answer. When she hasn't spoken in a couple of minutes, I tell her, "There's no pressure to give me an answer right now. Take as long as you want to think about it."

She looks up from her lap. "I trust you, Obsidian. Just like I did up on that turret, like I did in your car. Yes, I want to see what it's like."

Elation fills my bloodstream like the fizz of carbonation. I smile what feels like the first real smile I've had in decades. "Really?"

Her hand cups my cheek. "If I get to see this smile afterward."

I place my hand over hers, dwarfing it. "Do you want to?"

She nods. "It looks good on you."

My chest aches with how much emotion this woman tugs out of me. Almost as if I can't possibly contain it all. "Maybe I will then."

The urge to kiss her is so great that I almost succumb to temptation. But I haven't kissed a woman in over a decade, and I can't start with her. There'd be no coming back from it. I can't afford to be all in with this woman. Eventually, I'd break her. Apples never fall that far.

"It's agreed then. One night this week, and I won't tell you when, I'll come into your room while you're sleeping and do what I want to you."

She nods, a flicker of excitement in her eyes. "It's agreed."

I don't know how I don't pounce on her immediately, but somehow, I manage to stand from the couch and go behind my desk to start work for the day.

THREE NIGHTS LATER, I slip out of my bed at one in the morning. I didn't think I'd make it this many nights. I've been picturing taking Ariana as she sleeps. I've beat off to the idea of it ever since Ariana agreed.

Bare-chested in my gray lounge pants, I walk toward the bookcase in my bedroom and pull Edgar Allan Poe's *Fall of the House of Usher*. The whole bookcase slides to the side, revealing the hidden passageway tucked inside.

The east wing was my father's domain when he was alive, and it didn't shock me when I came across this passageway by accident years ago. He probably used it to sneak into my mother's room when she'd lock him out, before she moved to another wing at some point in their marriage. I'm not even sure if my brothers know it exists.

I light the candle I leave on the bookcase and turn back toward the entrance. Only sheer will allows me to enter the snug space, given the torture my father put me through as a child. But I overcame it years ago, unwilling to let him win and make me claustrophobic.

I count the doors I pass in the low light generated by the flickering candle, and when I reach the one that leads to Ariana's bedroom, I slowly push it open and walk through. She's snug in her bed and sound asleep, red hair draped across the pillow.

She looks so peaceful and young. Every one of the ten years between us seems amplified by the soft candlelight, her face and breathing relaxed.

After I set the candle on the bedside table, I slide my pants down my legs and step out of them. Standing at the edge of the bed, I watch her for a minute and stroke my cock, thinking of how fucking good it's going to feel when I sink into her.

In preparation, I bend down and slide the bottle of lube from the pocket of my lounge pants, then squirt some on my palm and stroke it over my dick. My goal isn't to hurt her. I wouldn't take any pleasure from doing so.

The bottle lands with a soft thud on top of my pants, and I slide onto the bed slowly so that I don't wake her. The blankets are already half off her body, and I can see that she's wearing just a T-shirt and underwear, like she was the morning she found me in the secret garden.

I bite my lip as I ease in behind her, careful not to wake her. She doesn't move an inch, and her breathing doesn't lose its natural, relaxed rhythm. My cock is painfully hard as I stare at her profile, gently pushing her underwear aside. She is blissfully unaware that I'm here. The fact that she's allowing me to do this is a gift she's offering me.

Fisting the base of my cock, I slide it between her folds until I feel her entrance, then I gently slide inside her with a satisfied sigh. A rush of endorphins floods through me.

It's as good as the first time I was inside her. Unlike the first time, though, I ease myself in and out, running one hand up under her T-shirt and feeling the weight of her breast in my palm. She makes a sound but doesn't move at first, then after a few more pumps inside her, she stiffens with a sharp inhale until she knows it's me. Her relaxation and the arch of her hips to give me access says how perfect she is for me. All without a word being said between us.

God, she's a fucking dream.

I release her breast and lift her leg, hooking it in the crook of my elbow before increasing my pace. The sounds of our labored breaths and twet slapping bounce off the walls. I nuzzle my face into her shock of red hair, inhaling her natural scent.

Her cunt is squeezing me so tight it's a wonder I haven't come. Sliding my other arm between her waist and the mattress, I bring my hand around until I find her mound and circle my fingers. A sharp rush of air slips through her lips, and her core flutters around my length.

We may not be kissing, but there's something intimate about what we're doing. We haven't spoken a word, but our bodies are speaking a language all their own under the glow of one flickering candle.

My strokes become longer, more forceful as I work her under my fingers until she's a wild, keening mess, desperate for what only I'm giving her.

The telltale tingle starts in my spine and centers in my groin, drawing up my balls. I apply more pressure until she detonates, stiffening and crying out. Her pussy milks my cock, and I bite her shoulder, unable to stop myself.

Neither of us moves or says a word, and after long minutes, I soften inside her and hear her breathing return to a relaxed rhythm as she falls back asleep.

I don't have the strength to leave as I probably should. Instead, I wrap one arm around her waist and drift off to sleep too.

TWENTY

ARIANA

I wake hours later with Obsidian's mouth between my legs.

Instinctively, my hand dives into the waves of the brown strands on top of his head, and he groans in approval when I tighten my grip. The morning light is just beginning to seep in through the windows, so I have a wonderful view of this god of a man between my legs.

My panties are gone, so he must have taken them off at some point after we had sex. The knowledge that he spilled inside me earlier and is now tasting the combination of our arousal is somehow hotter than if it were just me he was tasting.

He pushes two fingers into my depth while his tongue works magic on my clit. I'm so close to coming already that I have to wonder how long I stayed asleep after he started. When his fingers work me, it's less than a minute before my back arches off the mattress, and I climax. Obsidian's sure to lap up every drop before he kisses the inside of my thigh.

I wasn't sure what to expect when Obsidian explained his kink to me, other than that I was willing to see what I thought of it. But now that I've experienced it twice, I realize I like it more than I would have imagined.

The idea of being at this man's mercy, that he can take me whenever he sees fit, but knowing in my gut that he wouldn't hurt me, is a major turn-on. I know that every night when I go to bed from now on, I'll be wondering, "Is this the night he's going to visit me?"

He plops down beside me, resting his head in his hand and looking at me. "Good morning."

A lazy smile tilts my lips. "It is when it starts like that."

His gaze traces a path over my face, and there's something more relaxed about him this morning. "Does that mean you approve of last night and this morning?"

With a grin, I roll on top of him, straddling his lap. "More than approve. I want to do it again. And again. And again."

He looks up at me with something akin to wonder, and his length hardens under me. My eyes drift closed as I rock over his length, spreading the wetness between my legs all over him.

"That can be arranged." He threads his hand into the hair at the side of my head.

At this moment, I want to kiss him so badly. I want to feel his lips on mine, his tongue in my mouth. I wish he would kiss me. But I understand his reasoning. It's that one degree of separation between us that reminds me what this really is—two people using each other for sexual satisfaction.

Which also means I need to make the most of this while I have it.

I keep rocking, and though Obsidian's face heats with lust, there's also trepidation etched on it.

"Is everything okay?"

His Adam's apple bobs as he swallows. "I wanted to ask you something, but again, I don't know how you'll react."

I smirk at him. "It worked out well for us the first time." I reach down and grip the base of him.

He groans, and his hands go to my hips. "If I tell you, you can't tell anyone what we talked about. Ever." His voice is serious, as are his eyes now. He's not playing around.

"I won't. Nothing you ever tell me will leave these lips unless you say so." Positioning him at my entrance, I slowly ease myself down onto him.

We both groan in unison.

"Are you sure?" His eyes drift closed as I circle my hips. "I mean it. The consequences would be dire."

I have a flicker of hesitation, but I want him to tell me anyway. "I'm sure."

My head rocks back, and I place my hands behind me on his thighs, continuing to move up and down. He raises his head and watches where we're joined for a few moments, then he brings his thumb to my center and teases my clit. I sigh and rock my hips faster.

"There's this thing my brothers and I run. It's... unconventional."

"Okay." My voice is a thread of a whisper as I gasp from the attention he's giving me and the feel of his girth stretching me in the best way.

"It's a sex club."

My movements stop, and I think of what I saw at the manor that one Saturday, the SUVs driving through town, the mask that woman wore.

I start moving again. "And you want me to join you there?"

Relief coats his face, and I'm pretty sure it's because I didn't climb off him. "Yes. But it's not like other clubs. The Ritual Room is members only, and its members are the most elite people in the world."

That gives me pause. Now I understand what he meant when he said that if I told anyone, the consequences would be dire. Those people don't mess around with their secrets, and I have no doubt that anyone with loose lips is dealt with swiftly and permanently, Uma-style.

Obsidian speeds up his thumb, and I slam myself down on him one last time as my orgasm takes hold of me and doesn't let go for several long, blissful moments.

I pause to catch my breath, and Obsidian sits up, his six-pack abs contracting under my fingertips. He takes the hem of my T-shirt and pulls it up off my body, then wraps his arms around me and drags me back down so my soft chest is pressed against his hard one.

"There's an initiation you'd have to go through to join," he says, slamming into me from below. "Everyone wears masks, but you'd have to be unmasked your first night, and you'd be filmed as leverage."

"What would I have to do?" My voice vibrates from the force of his thrusts.

"Whatever I want."

Those words send a delicious thrill through me. I tuck my face into his neck on the side with the wolf tattoo. "Which is?"

"I'm not sure yet. My brothers and I are the only ones with access to the tapes, though."

I cry out when he slams inside me and holds himself there for a second before doing it over and over.

"You don't have to decide now. Give me your answer when you're ready." He turns his head and bites my shoulder.

The pain mixed with the pleasure is divine. I pull away from his neck and bring my face over his so he can see me answer his question. My hair hangs down around our faces like a curtain of flames. "I want to join. I want to do this with you."

At my words, he comes on a cry, holding himself inside me until I stop feeling his cock twitching, and he's spent.

His hands cradle my face. "Are you sure? You don't have to say yes. We can just keep doing what we're doing here."

"I'm sure, Obsidian. I don't even need to think about it. I want it all with you." The words slip from my lips before I can stop them.

But rather than retreat, he tugs me back down to his chest and squeezes me tightly.

I am such a goner for this man, kissing or not. Sex only or not. And though falling hard for someone would elate most women, all I can think about is what's going to happen when my father's debt is settled, and I have to leave him behind.

CHAPTER
TWENTY-ONE

The next morning, I arrange a meeting with my brothers. Since the four of us all run the Ritual Room, I need to give them the heads-up that I'll be initiating Ariana at the next meeting. I also asked for Asher and Kol's wives, Anabelle and Rapsody, to be here, and Nero's girlfriend, Cinder. They're as much a part of this as my brothers are. Plus, I think they'll be on my side if any of my brothers try to give me a hard time about wanting to bring in Ariana.

The mood is tense when I walk into Asher's office and find the six of them already there. I'm not sure what they think I'm going to spring on them, but they clearly don't think it's good news.

"Thanks for taking the time to meet with me this morning," I say after I've closed the office door.

"This can't be good," Kol mumbles, his hand linked with Rapsody's.

"And why's that?" I ask, not bothering to sit.

"You're starting in like you're at the head of a boardroom table—lubing us up before you really fuck us up the ass."

I set my hands on my hips. "Fine. I'll get right to the point then. I'll be initiating Ariana into the Ritual Room at the next meeting."

A stunned silence fills the room.

"You're sleeping with your assistant?" Asher says, clearly unimpressed.

I narrow my eyes at him. "Are you of all people really asking me that question?" I look at Anabelle.

Her cheeks go red, and she shrugs.

"What happened to wanting to get rid of her?" Kol asks.

I'm unwilling to explain to everyone the pull I feel toward her, so I don't answer him.

"You know what it means if you bring her in," Asher warns.

"She's here to stay then? You care about her that much?" Nero asks.

I can't tell them the truth—that we have a deal that doesn't involve emotions. They'd never clear her to join. So I have to lie. The rest will work itself out. Why should I be the only one of the four of us who can't have the person they want there with them?

"I know what it means," I confirm with a nod.

Kol stands from where he sits beside Rapsody on the couch and walks over to grip my shoulder. "I'm happy for you, Sid. You deserve this."

All the women have big smiles and trade comments about how they can't wait to get to know Ariana and how she must really be special if I want to initiate her.

Jesus, the way they're reacting, you'd think I just told them I'm engaged.

Nero walks over with a huge smile. "This is a good thing. Don't look so uncomfortable."

The only reason I'm uncomfortable is because of how things went down between us before I took off. I haven't really seen much of him, but I realize now that I owe both him and Cinder an apology.

"Listen..." I shove my hands into the pockets of my suit pants. "What happened before all the shit went down with you and Cinder, and I took off..."

The smile drops from his face, and he becomes serious. "I know you were in a bad way, brother. Don't worry about it."

I nod. He knows our history, my past, and I'm grateful to him for letting me off easy and not making me grovel. "I appreciate that, but I still need to apologize to your girlfriend."

Nero gives me an appreciative smile that tells me all is really forgiven now, and he calls Cinder over to join us. She does, if a bit apprehensively.

"Cinder, I just wanted to apologize for the things I said to you before. My head wasn't in a good place, but regardless, I should never have said them. I hope you can forgive me."

She doesn't put up a fight, just smiles and draws me into a hug, which I return even if I just pat her back and never step all the way into the hug. "I appreciate the apology. Let's start fresh, okay?"

She pulls away, and I nod.

I chat with Nero and Cinder for another minute before I excuse myself, saying I need to get back to my office to start my day. Before I go, I step over to Asher, who's standing on his own, leaning against the mantle of the oversized fireplace, hands in his pockets, observing the rest of us.

He doesn't look away from everyone else as I approach. "Who would have ever thought this was possible?"

My forehead creases. "What do you mean?"

He spares me a glance. "Look around, Sid. How long has it been since this place was filled with anything but hurt and sorrow, misery and violence?"

I follow his gaze to the sight of them laughing with each other and chatting easily without an ulterior motive. My gut churns because I'm still not a part of it. Not really.

My brothers have found their life partners, but I can never be that to someone. If I even tried, I'd end up hurting and destroying them. There's too much of my father in me for any other outcome, and I refuse to do that to the person who's supposed to mean the most to me.

I clear my throat. "Yeah, I see what you mean."

It's all I can offer him. I've already lied to them today by making them think that Ariana is the end game for me. I don't have it in me to double down on the lie.

But Asher being Asher, he picks up on my little avoidance tactic. "Something wrong, Sid?"

I shake my head. "No, it's just a lot, you know."

Understanding flits in his blue eyes. "It is. Especially when you were raised the way we were. But you'll get used to it. Learn to trust it."

I nod, because what else can I do? "I need to get back to my office. Have to finish going over the contract Havis Corp sent over for the acquisition."

"Let me know if anything seems amiss."

"Should be fine. The team's been over it already, but I just want to be sure. See you later."

He nods, then joins Anabelle.

I leave his office with anticipation firing in my veins, eager to brainstorm all the ways I can initiate Ariana next weekend, but at the same time, there's a lump in my throat. Because despite all the changes in my life, I still carry around a piece of the feeling I had on that stormy beach—that I'm not meant to have what my brothers have found.

WITH ONE FINAL THRUST, I push into Ariana and hold myself there, spilling inside her.

Her hands skim over the scars dotting my back, but she doesn't ask about them. Hasn't asked about them, thankfully.

Leaning in, I kiss her neck, then I roll off of her, throwing my arm up over my head, and work to control my breathing.

Since our deal was struck, we haven't been able to get enough of each other. I feel as if I'm a slave to an addiction because even minutes after I've come inside her, I want her again.

She groans next to me, and I roll over to face her, lying on my side with my head in my palm.

"I have to go shower and get ready."

I frown. "Where are you going?"

She rolls over to face me. "It's Saturday night. I'm going to meet my brother."

Fuck. I had so many other plans for her and for her body tonight. "Does he visit you every weekend?"

She stills at my question and alarms flare red in my mind. "We're close. We both still lived with my dad before I came here."

Ariana hasn't said much about how she grew up, but the little she has said, and knowing that her mother took off on her, makes me think it wasn't an easy upbringing. I know better than anyone how trauma can bond siblings.

I want to ask her more questions: Where is she from? What was her childhood like? What's her brother like? But I'm trying hard to stick to what we've agreed to, and knowing more personal details about her will only make it more difficult.

"Well, make sure you tell him you're unavailable next Saturday."

She gives me a questioning look.

"It's your initiation into the Ritual Room."

Her eyes widen.

"Having second thoughts?" I try to keep my voice casual as though it wouldn't matter to me either way, but I feel the panic course through me.

"Not at all. I'm just nervous, not sure what to expect."

I kiss her shoulder. "Expect to be satisfied."

She hums low in her throat, and my dick twitches to life where it's pressed against her thigh. A rich, hearty laugh escapes her, and I pull back to enjoy the sight of her amusement.

"Again? Already?"

I grin at her. "What can I say? You make me insatiable."

With that proclamation, she rolls away from me and slides out of bed. "Well then, I better flee while I can."

I enjoy the sight of her naked body. Her perky breasts with dusty pink nipples, the way her waist nips in, and the swell of her hips. The tiny patch of red between her thighs. Everything about her is tailor made to draw me in.

Ariana slips on the shorts and shirt she had on earlier before I divested her of them.

"You sure you have to go?" I stroke my half-hard cock.

Her eyes heat, but then her mood shifts, and she turns away. "I do. Believe me, I'd much rather stay here in bed with you."

"Maybe I'll sneak into your room while you're sleeping…"

The offer hangs, knowing she'll understand the implication.

She bites her lower lip. "I'd like that."

I nod, my dick growing even harder in my hand. "I'll see you later then."

She walks toward the bedroom door, granting me a smile over her shoulder before she leaves me with a damn hard-on.

CHAPTER
TWENTY-TWO

It's the night of the initiation, and I haven't been this nervous in a long time.

Probably not since the day I went to see Uma.

My brother wasn't pleased when I told him I wouldn't be able to meet him this week. When he asked why, I lied and told him I had to be out of town for work. There's no way I'm admitting to him that I'm sleeping with Obsidian. He'd see right through me and know that I feel more than sexual attraction for the man.

And I can't tell him about the Ritual Room, that's for certain.

Obsidian explained to me how things would go tonight—we'll arrive and proceed to a dais in the main room. I'll be the only one unmasked, and I have to do whatever he asks of me, though I'm not to know prior to arriving what that might be. Apparently, every meeting has a theme, and this month's theme is Mardi Gras Madness.

I slip into the outfit Obsidian left with me earlier today, if you can call it that. It's a sequined purple, yellow, and green bikini bottom, some strappy gold heels, a matching sequined headband with feathers sticking out the top, and beads. Lots and lots of beaded necklaces that will act as a shirt of sorts, covering my breasts.

Not that I have any reason to think anything about tonight will be modest, but I'm glad I don't have to walk in there completely naked from the get-go.

There's a knock at the door. I survey myself quickly in the mirror before going to answer it. I swing the door open and come up short at Obsidian. He's always impeccably dressed, and tonight is no different.

He's wearing a deep green suit with a *fleur-de-lis* design in gold sequins on the jacket. He hasn't bothered to put on a shirt underneath.

But none of that is what makes me draw up short. It's the wolf mask. It's gold and vicious looking, the top two canine teeth extending down as if in warning.

His dark eyes take me in through the mask, and though I can't see his face, I see the approval in his eyes. "You ready for this?"

"I'm nervous, but ready."

He steps into me, and when our chests meet, it makes the necklaces shift, some cresting over my nipples in the most delicious way.

"You're going to be amazing. I have no doubt."

He takes my hand, and we leave my bedroom. He leads me through the house, out of the east wing. I get a little turned around, but eventually we end up in front of a carved wooden door.

Obsidian removes a skeleton key from the pocket of his pants and unlocks the door, swinging it open. On the other side is a set of stone stairs that lead down. The entire thing looks as if it's been carved from the earth. Old sconces flicker on one side, but I can't see all the way down to the bottom.

Setting aside my unease, I start down the steps. I trust Obsidian, and though it's absolutely creepy as heck down here, my steps don't slow. When we're close to the bottom, the thrumming of music comes from somewhere. By the time we reach the last step, sensual music fills the space.

We're at the end of a long hallway interspersed with closed doors. I can see people mingling at the end in what appears to be the main room.

Obsidian takes my hand again and wastes no time leading me down the hallway. As we draw closer, people seem to notice our arrival. The hum of conversation underlying the music dies down, then stops entirely when we step into the opening that leads to a huge room with a domed ceiling made from stone.

It's filled with people in costumes that suit the theme. They're all wearing masks, either black, red, or white, except... I notice a few gold masks. When I see the one with the bear on it, I realize that must be Asher. At least I assume so, given that he has that bear tattoo on his hand.

Until this moment, I didn't give much thought to the fact that Obsidian's brothers and their partners would be here. Will it be embarrassing as hell if I come upon them in the manor after this?

I push aside my worry. Now isn't the time for it.

Obsidian seems to wait for a beat, then a path forms in the crowd, and he leads me down it.

I feel exposed with my bare back, wearing just the necklaces. Exposed, but my nipples pebble from the sensation of all their eyes roaming my skin.

When the crowd parts all the way to the stairs at the side of the dais, I get my first look at what's waiting for me. It's a massage table. It's not until I step onto the stage that I realize there's a hole in the table at about waist length. I realize then what it is.

It's a milking table.

Heat blooms between my thighs. Somehow Obsidian knows, because he looks at me with a smirk before he turns to address the room.

"In true Mardi Gras fashion, I feel it's only right that Ariana offers you her beads before the show begins." He gestures for me to take a spot at his side at the edge of the dais. "Anyone who'd like a necklace is welcome to come grab one."

I suck in a breath and watch as a man wearing a red mask steps forward. I'm not sure what to expect. Will he touch me or just take the necklace? Obsidian and I haven't discussed anything like that.

He approaches, and I watch his gaze dip and take in my body. The heat from his eyes causes fire to blossom between my legs. He removes one of the necklaces from over my head. I bend forward to make it easier for him, exposing my breasts to anyone at my sides.

Next a woman approaches, and she looks as interested as the man is. I'm not into women, but her obvious appreciation for my body churns something between my thighs.

I stand at the edge of the dais and bend my head every time someone approaches. It feels like an unraveling, an unwrapping. How Obsidian knew I would need something gradual like this to ease me in, I have no idea. But I suppose I shouldn't be surprised. That man has been attuned to my needs since the moment he first put his hand under my dress in his car. With the weight of each necklace that disappears from around my neck, it feels as if I'm shedding some of my trepidation.

Finally, Obsidian takes the last two necklaces, pulling them over his own head until they rest on his chest. I stand topless in front of a room full of strangers, yet I've never felt more confident. Especially when I see pride, adoration, and lust in Obsidian's eyes.

"Undress me." His voice reverberates over the music, and I step forward.

First, I undo the jacket and slide it over his shoulders until it falls to the floor behind him. Next, I get on my haunches and help him out of his shoes, setting them aside. I settle on my knees and undo his belt buckle, then the button on his pants. My nipples are hard points as I undo the zipper and see he's wearing no underwear. Using my hands, I maneuver the pants over the globes of his muscled ass until they pool at his ankles. Then I set them aside with his shoes, stand, and wait for my next instructions.

My breaths come in short, shallow spurts as Obsidian trails his hand down his body until his hand wraps around his thick cock.

"Do you know what that is?" He nods toward the table.

"A milking table."

A small smile tilts his lips. "Do you know what to do if I go lie on it?"

I nod. "Yes." My voice is needy. The idea of pleasing him in that way in front of all of these people, of having them witness the connection between us... I'm eager.

"Good."

He steps forward and threads a hand through the hair at the side of my head. For a moment, I think he might lean in and kiss me. Instead, he brings his forehead down to meet mine and breathes me in before turning to lie on the table.

It's the first really good look I've gotten of the circular scars dotting his back. I've felt them plenty in the throes of passion, but never had an unobstructed view. My chest squeezes painfully because it's obvious this is something that was inflicted upon him, and I can only imagine the horror of having to live with visible scars of torture.

I try not to let any of that show in my face when he looks at me before lowering himself face down onto the table. I crawl under the table and see that he's fitted his cock through the opening. Liquid fire erupts in my belly. I know it's Obsidian I take in hand, but I can't see him. I'm one step removed from him, and there's something so tawdry about it that it makes my core tighten.

With my fist wrapped around his girth, I slide my hand down his length and bring my mouth up to the crown. I suck gently on it and whirl my tongue around the tip, continuing to stroke him with my hand. Then I pull back and run my hand all the way down, spreading my saliva over his entire length.

I work him like that, every so often changing my stroking pattern so he won't know what to expect. When I bring my free hand up to his balls and squeeze, he moans loudly enough that I can hear him over the music.

He can't thrust in my mouth like this, but I know if this table weren't here, he would be. Knowing he's at my mercy makes it even hotter. My pussy clenches around nothing, desperate to be filled by him.

Hearing Obsidian moan again urges me on. I keep jerking his stiff cock while I bring my mouth up to his balls, sucking one then the other. He barks out a curse, and I can tell he's close from the usual tremor in his voice right before he comes.

The power trip pleasing him gives me is nothing I've ever felt before. Never would I have thought I could bring a man like Obsidian to his knees, but he is absolutely at my mercy. When I glance away from him and see people in the crowd fondling themselves or each other, the power skyrockets inside me.

I redouble my efforts, returning my mouth to his dick and

using my hands to play with his now slippery balls. It doesn't take long before his precum touches my tongue.

"I want to come on your tits."

Pulling my lips away from him, I jerk him until he comes with a fierce bellow, then I squeeze every last drop out of him.

I'm not even the one who came, but my breathing is ragged, my adrenaline high. When I feel him pull away, I release his shaft and remain where I am until his hand appears below the table to help me out from under it. I take it, and once I'm standing in front of him, his gaze dips down to my chest.

"Always such a good fucking girl." He swipes through his arousal with two fingers and brings them to my mouth.

I open for him and hum around his finger at the salty taste of his release, not diverting my gaze from his dark one. Then before I know what's happening, he's dipped down and lifted me over his shoulder.

It was hot the first time he did it in the tower, but it feels even more so now as I see the feet of the crowd part around him as we make our exit. At first, I think he's taking me to one of the rooms down the hall—he mentioned that he has his own private room—but when I see the stairs appear, I realize that's not the case.

We enter the manor. I hear him swing the large wooden door closed behind us, and he only takes a few strides before he says, "Fuck it," and he lowers me to the floor. "I can't wait until we get back to my room."

Before I can say or do anything, he spins me around and plasters me against the wall. We're in the middle of the manor, I'm half naked and he's totally naked, yet I don't want him to stop. All I want is him and whatever he'll give me.

Obsidian rips my bottoms from my body, lifts one of my legs under the crook of his arm to spread me, and with one brutal thrust, he's inside me. I cry out, and my hands grasp aimlessly at the wall as he pounds into me.

"What are you doing to me? What kind of spell have you put over me?" he seethes into my ear.

The sound of him slamming into me echoes down the hallway. He pushes his free hand into my hair, wrenching my head back and forcing me to meet his dark gaze.

"What is this?" His pupils are blown, and fear and disbelief mixes with lust in his eyes.

"I don't know," I admit. "I just know I can't get enough."

He cries out and releases my head, fucking me so hard, I'll be sore for days. He's feral, unstrained, and animalistic. Having his way with me is about nothing more than sating his desire. Exerting his dominance over me. And I love it. I love it so much that I come without him ever touching my clit.

I cry out, my body spasming between him and the wall. With one last savage thrust, he fills me, snarling at my neck right before biting down, sure to leave a mark.

It's wild and untamed and perfect.

CHAPTER
TWENTY-THREE

ARIANA

Obsidian slides out of me and leads me through the manor by the hand, all while his lust spills down the insides of my thighs. It's only now, after we've finished, that I'm worried and embarrassed that we might run into someone from the staff. I certainly wasn't worried about it while he was fucking the life out of me.

Thankfully, we reach his room without seeing a soul. He doesn't bother closing the door, going straight to the en suite, and turns on the shower. Concern swims in his gaze when his eyes meet mine.

"What's wrong?" I step forward and rest my hand on his chest.

He pushes his hand through his soaked hair with a wince. "I was too rough with you. I'm sorry."

"Obsidian, I'm fine." I push back the sweaty hair that's fallen over his forehead.

"No, I hurt you. You must be sore."

"A little, but I liked it. If I didn't, I would have asked you to stop."

His gaze bounces around my face, unable to settle anywhere, but the pain in his eyes cuts me.

"Hey." I bring both hands to the stubble on his cheeks and cradle his face. "You didn't do anything wrong. I would have spoken up if I wasn't into it. If I'm honest, it turns me on so much when you can't control yourself around me. I'm not just saying that." I tip his head down to see the truth of my words in my face.

Tears gather in the corners of his eyes. "If I hurt you... I couldn't bear it, Ariana. Couldn't bear it if I were that kind of a monster."

Dropping my hands from his face, I wrap my arms around his waist and hug him as hard as I can. "You're not a monster, Obsidian."

His arms settle around me, and he nudges his face in the crook of my neck. "I don't know what is about you, I can't get enough."

I squeeze my eyes shut and hold him for long minutes, my emotions running ragged in my chest and flaying me from the inside out. We may have made a deal that feelings wouldn't be involved, but it's clear to me now that was never going to be the case. Even if neither of us ever admits it, there's more between us than an insane amount of sexual chemistry.

"Are you ready to get in the shower?" I eventually ask when steam fills the room.

He nods against the crook of my neck. "Yeah." His voice cracks.

When I pull away, some of the pain in his eyes has dimmed, but he's still locked in his head.

"C'mon." I slide my hand in his and lead him inside the huge walk-in shower.

This is the first time we've showered together. It's the first time I've showered with any man, and I treasure the fact Obsidian gets this first.

There's more than one shower head, so we step under separate ones. The warm water relaxes my sore muscles and eases their fatigue. We're both quiet, and as the silence stretches between us, my thoughts drift to something I was wondering earlier today.

"Have you ever initiated anyone into the club before?"

Obsidian's head turns in my direction with a scowl. "Why would you ask that?"

I shrug. "Just wondering if this is a semi-regular Saturday night for you. Wondering how many women are at the Ritual Room because you brought them in."

He breaks the distance between us and wraps his hand around the back of my neck, dipping his head so our eyes line up. "I've never invited another woman to join. And I never will again. You're my first and only."

When he says things like that, I wish I could stay here forever and love this man, but once he finds out why I'm here or what I've stolen from him, he won't look at me like he is right now. As if I'm a woman he could love too.

I don't bother asking the other question I was wondering—how many women there he's slept with. I won't like the answer, and I don't want it to be my main focus the next time I'm down there.

Inching up to my tippy toes, I lick his wolf tattoo then place a light kiss on his neck. "Good answer." I pick up the shampoo.

"Here, let me." He waves his hand toward him.

I place the bottle in his hand and turn around. Seconds later, he massages shampoo into my hair, and a moan escapes me from his fingers kneading my scalp as the shower fills with his scent. He rinses the shampoo out of my hair and applies conditioner.

"Was tonight what you thought it would be?" he asks.

I'm not surprised he's waited until my back is to him to ask. It's a concern of his and shows his vulnerability. Something he guards with a thick concrete wall.

"I'm not sure I really knew what to expect. But my nerves went away faster than I thought. I don't think I expected to be so turned on by everyone watching."

His deep chuckle sounds from behind me as he finger-combs the conditioner through my hair. "Maybe you're an exhibitionist."

"Would that bother you?"

He places his hands on my shoulders, turning me around. "Ariana, this isn't just about my sexual satisfaction. If there's something you're into, something you want to try, all you have to do is ask."

I nod and smile. "All right, turn around while this soaks into my hair so I can shampoo yours."

He does as I ask, and I pick up the shampoo bottle. I'm pouring the shampoo into my palm, my eyes fixated on his scars. I've felt them but never seen them so close up. He's never told me how he got them, and I'm not going to push him—he'll tell me when he's ready. I'm not sure I have a right to know such intimate details about him given that I'm keeping my entire history from him.

Regardless, I place a kiss on one. He stiffens for a fraction of a second, but he doesn't turn around or tell me to stop, so I follow the path to the next one, then the next and the next. It's my way of telling him that I care for all the parts of him, even the broken ones.

Once I've worshipped each round scar, I wash his hair. Neither of us speaks about my act, and we remain quiet, contemplative until we step out of the shower to dry off.

Obsidian invites me to spend the night in his bed, and as I curl up against his chest and let the steady thrum of his heart lull me to sleep, I only have one wish—to take his pain away.

WHEN I WAKE SOMETIME in the middle of the night, there's a loneliness nestled in my chest, and I'm not surprised when my hand reaches to an empty spot next to me. Sure enough, when I open my eyes and roll over, his side of the bed is bare. The bed sheets are cold to the touch, so he's been gone for some time.

I sit up, wondering if I should seek him out. Thinking back on how quiet and withdrawn he was earlier, I want to make sure he's okay. But where to start looking? Could I find my way back to the secret garden? I'm not so sure. This manor is huge.

First, I go to my room to slide on sandals and put on shorts and a T-shirt. I was lucky earlier that no one came upon us, but I don't want to risk it again. Then I make my way through the manor. I don't find him, but I didn't think I would.

As soon as I step outside into the dark, I regret not bringing my phone to use the flashlight. Fog swirls around my feet, the tendrils reminding me of hands rising from the earth like phantoms ready to drag me down. Suppressing a shiver, I'm thankful for the almost-full moon. The ivy-covered wall rises up in front of me almost out of nowhere, and the iron gate leading into the garden is ajar.

Please be here.

Suddenly, the memory of Obsidian in that ocean flickers to mind, and a flood of anxiety rushes through me. I don't think he was so distraught that he'd consider ending his life, but there's so much he still keeps from me. Showing weakness isn't something he's comfortable with.

My footsteps speed up, uncaring if I trip and fall. I need to set eyes on him and know that he's okay. I rush through the gate and immediately look over to where I found him that night and breathe a sigh of relief at his figure sitting in the dark.

Thank God.

He doesn't seem to hear me approach until I'm mere feet from him, but his face shows no surprise when his eyes meet mine.

"Hey," I say in a quiet voice, afraid I'm disturbing him.

"Hey."

"Everything okay?" I sit beside him and place a hand on his thigh.

Obsidian blows out a breath. "Just couldn't sleep. My mind was racing." He gives me a lame attempt at a smile, a forced one I've never seen before.

"Want to talk about it?"

His gaze drifts over to the spot where I'm assuming his mother's lifeless body was discovered. "Not really, no."

I pretend my heart isn't cracking from him not trusting me, but I remind myself I'm not being open with him either.

We sit in silence for a long time, listening to the sounds of the night. What was once disturbing is now comforting. The mist at my feet, the man at my side, and the hanging moon overhead.

After some time, I want to draw him out of his spiraling thoughts. "Can I ask about the wolf tattoo? You told me why you got it on such a visible spot, but you never told me why a wolf."

He gives me a resigned smile. "My mother coined each of her sons a different animal. I was the wolf. She said I was resilient, loyal with fierce instincts, and that I was territorial and would always look out for my pack."

I didn't know the woman, but I can understand exactly why she referred to him as such.

"Each of my brothers has their own tattoo in kind. You've probably noticed Asher's."

"The bear."

"Yeah. Kol has a lion, and Nero a raven. I don't know how she saw so much of who we were at such a young age."

I grab his hand, and his palm swallows mine. "It's nice that you still have memories of her. I have very few memories of my mother."

He squeezes my hand and looks back at that spot again. He stands quickly. "I need to go for a ride."

I have no idea where he wants to go in the middle of the night, but I don't want to leave him alone when he's feeling like this, so I stand and block out the fact he might never feel comfortable showing me his vulnerable side. "Lead the way."

And he does. He takes us to a garage that's separate from the main manor, one I didn't know existed. When we're inside, I walk toward his Rolls Royce, but he says, "This way."

I stop in my tracks when he pulls a motorcycle helmet off a shelf and holds it out for me.

"A motorcycle?" My voice must highlight my fear because he walks toward me and places the helmet over my head.

"I take it you've never been on one before?" He adjusts the strap under my chin.

I shake my head, clenching my hands to still them.

"All you have to do is hold on to me tight and lean into the turns." He fits his own helmet on his head and walks toward a sports bike. Obsidian straddles the bike and gestures for me to sit behind him.

My stomach is in my throat as I walk toward what I'm afraid will be my doom. Once I'm on, I wrap my arms around his middle and hold on as tightly as possible, not caring that we haven't even moved an inch yet.

He starts the bike, then squeezes my hand as if in reassurance before we're off. Obsidian takes it easy as we make our way off the property, but once we're past the iron gates, we rocket down the road.

I squeeze my eyes shut, terrified, until he slows to take a corner, and I do as he says, leaning into the turn. Once we've straightened, we burst forward, accelerating at a pace I didn't know was possible, and I realize this is another one of Obsidian's death-defying efforts to forget the past and live in the moment, to feel alive with adrenaline surging through his veins.

Hasn't he figured it out yet? No matter how fast this bike can go, he can't outrun his demons.

CHAPTER

TWENTY-FOUR

ARIANA

By Monday morning, Obsidian was a little more himself, and now on Wednesday, there's no trace of the forlorn man who appeared after he fucked me in the middle of the manor.

When there's a knock on the office door midway through the day, it startles me at first because very rarely does anyone come by during the workday. I look up and see Anabelle looking around the office, presumably searching for Obsidian.

"Hi, you just missed him. He went to grab a cappuccino from the kitchen. Apparently, Mrs. Potter makes the best ones."

She rolls her eyes good-naturedly. "Asher feels the same about the green smoothies she makes him in the morning. We'll never compete." She laughs.

I stand from my desk and walk toward her. "Do you want to wait, or I can pass along a message if you like?"

"Actually, I'm here to see you. I wanted to see what you're up to tonight."

Surprised, I blink several times. "Um… I didn't have anything planned."

"Great! The girls and I want to take you out for a drink so we can get to know you better."

Alarm bells blare in my head because why do they want to get to know me? "The girls?"

"Kol's wife, Rapsody, and Nero's girlfriend, Cinder."

I nod. "Should I be concerned?"

I try to keep my voice light, but I'm honestly worried. Maybe they're digging for information, and if so, why? Has someone figured out what I'm doing? Maybe Asher asked her to pry because girl talk usually divulges more.

No, if that were the case, I'd already be out on my ass.

She waves off my question. "Not at all. You're a part of Sid's life now, and we just want to welcome you into the inner circle, that's all." She looks behind her and leans closer. "We all know firsthand how challenging the Voss men can be." She winks.

Though I'm nervous about what questions might come up and what I'll do to avoid the truth, the idea of making some friends while I'm here sounds too nice to decline. We moved around so much when I was young that I never had the opportunity to form any close female relationships. "In that case, I'd love to. What time were you thinking?"

"Be ready to go at eight. Meet us at the front door, and one of the drivers will take us into town so no one has to worry about driving."

I nod. "Will do. Thanks for the invite."

Sid walks through the door and halts when he sees I'm not alone. "Anabelle. Asher being unbearable? Need me to straighten him out?" He sips his cappuccino and continues toward his desk.

"It's funny that you think anyone can straighten that man out," she says with a humorous lilt. "I was just inviting Ariana out for girls' night tonight. Well, I'd better get back to work. Don't want the boss firing me." She winks, turns on her heel, and leaves.

Obsidian stares at me, chewing on his cheek.

"Did you want me to turn down her invitation?" I ask him.

"Not at all."

But his words don't match the look on his face.

WE SETTLE IN A BOOTH, and I sit next to Anabelle with Rapsody and Cinder across from us. Rapsody has a blond chin-length bob and is about as sweet as they come, while Cinder has big blue eyes and long blond hair styled with a wave. I feel a kinship with Cinder instantly, as if we've both seen some shit in our lives.

I'm anxious about being here with someone other than my brother, as though they're closer to discovering my secret by sheer proximity to where our exchanges go down. But the bartender isn't the one I'm used to seeing on Saturday nights, so at least I don't need to worry about her calling out my frequent visits in front of the girls.

Cinder takes our drink requests, then goes over to the bar.

"She used to work here," Anabelle says.

She and Rapsody laugh when they see the surprise on my face.

"None of us come from money," Anabelle adds.

I don't know why I assumed they did, but it just seemed most likely. Don't the Voss brothers kind stay in their own pond?

"How did you all meet them?" I look between her and Rapsody.

"I met Kol while my mother was in the hospital. He was there visiting someone," Rapsody says.

I get the distinct sense that there's more to Rapsody's story, but I'm not going to pry since I don't want them to pry into my own.

"And I met Asher when I came to work for him. Kinda like you and Sid." Anabelle knocks her shoulder with mine.

"I never expected…"

"Oh, we know," Anabelle says. "There's just something that draws you in about those Voss men, isn't there?"

My cheeks heat. I realize as I'm sitting here talking to them that they would have been there the night of my initiation. I don't know why I didn't think of that until now.

"Were you guys there the night I..." I glance around the bar. "In the basement?"

Both women give me a sympathetic look and nod.

"It's only weird if you make it weird," Anabelle says.

Right. Maybe I shouldn't have brought it up.

"I'd never done anything like that before," I admit.

"Oh, neither had we," Rapsody says.

Cinder returns and sets the drinks on the table, sliding my glass of wine over to me. Normally I'd order a beer, but I felt like maybe I should order something a little more sophisticated in front of these ladies. Although now that I've chatted with them, I don't think it would have mattered.

"What are we talking about?" Cinder asks before taking a sip of her drink.

Rapsody whispers the answer in Cinder's ear.

"Ah, gotcha," she smiles. "Will you be returning next month?"

I nod. "Yeah, as long as Obsidian wants me there." I bring the wine glass to my lips.

"I was just saying how none of us had ever done anything like that before," Rapsody fills Cinder in.

"Yes and no for me. I used to strip for a living. That's actually where I met Nero." I appreciate the fact that there's zero shame in Cinder's tone. "But I'd never, you know, in front of other people."

Cinder is very well-endowed, and I can imagine that she must've done well when she worked at the strip club.

"I never would have guessed that," I say.

She shrugs. "None of us really met the guys in a conventional way. But that doesn't mean it can't be something good."

I twirl my glass by the stem. "Why do I get the feeling that's directed at me?"

Anabelle squeezes my hand. "You'll have to excuse our excitement. It's just that none of us have ever seen Sid into a woman like he is with you, and from what the guys say, he's never been serious with anyone else."

"How do you know he's serious about me?" I take another sip of my wine to ground myself.

Anabelle gives me a look of disbelief. "He wouldn't have initiated you into the club if he wasn't serious, Ariana. They only do that for the keepers."

Is that true? Does Obsidian see a future with me despite never having said that?

And if so, why do I feel both happy and sad at the idea of it?

But I know the answer to that question—it's because there can be no future for us. As soon as he figures out what and who I really am, he's going to hate me.

I try to play off their enthusiasm. "We'll see." Wanting to change the subject from Obsidian and me, I turn to Rapsody. "So what do you do?"

We chat for a while longer, finishing another drink before Anabelle says, "We should probably call it a night. Asher has an early phone call I need to be up for." She pulls out her phone and texts the driver to pick us up.

"This was really fun. Thank you for inviting me." I polish off the rest of my wine.

"You should have your meals with us in the dining room," Cinder says.

Though I think I'd like that, I'm not sure how Obsidian would feel about it. "I think I'll wait until Obsidian invites me, but I appreciate the invite, thanks."

"I get ya," she says, and we all slide out of the booth.

After Cinder says a quick goodbye to the bartender, we head outside to the car waiting for us.

Before we all go to our separate wings in the manor, each woman gives me a hug goodbye. I can't imagine being a part of this life. A real part of Obsidian's and their lives. It would be a dream, but who am I kidding? A life like this isn't in the cards for me. It's going to be hard when I have to leave them all.

CHAPTER

TWENTY-FIVE

ARIANA

Something wakes me.

At first I think it's just because of the few drinks at the bar—I never sleep well when I've drank—but the bedside light illuminates a trail of sand beside the bed to the bedroom door.

A chill steals over me. It's happening again. I want to ignore it, sweep it away, but just as the last time, a feeling in my gut tells me to follow the sand.

I place the book I was reading when I drifted off on the bedside table and slide out of bed. As soon as I take the first step toward the door, it's as if there's a lasso around my chest, and a power stronger than me is tugging me forward. As always, the hallway is filled with shadows. That feeling of being watched crawls up my spine, but I follow the trail of sand all the way to the end of the hall and to the door that leads to the turret.

The big wooden door is swung wide open and the sand leads up the stairs, so I begin the arduous trek up and around the circular staircase. When I reach the landing at the top, the door there is open as well, and the sand ends at the threshold. Clearly, Obsidian is here since all the doors are open. Is he leaving the sand for me to follow since each time it's led me to him?

When I step into the room, I find him in one of the old chairs, holding the glass that stores the sand from his last vacation with his mother. He doesn't look up as I make my way over to him. Everything about him—the tension in his face, the slump of his shoulders, the way he's staring at what he's holding—screams the pain that inflicts this man daily.

All I want is to take that pain away. I'm desperate to help him, but I don't know how. Especially since he doesn't allow me in.

I stand in front of him, but he still doesn't tear his gaze away from the glass jar. "Obsidian."

His gaze lifts to my face, and his eyes are sad, so sad, and so tired.

Without his permission, I crawl into his lap, wanting to console him. "What's wrong?" My hand cups his cheek, turning his head so our eyes meet.

"I don't want to be like him," he whispers.

My forehead creases. "Who?"

"My father." He wraps his arms around me and squeezes me into his body, still holding the glass jar with one hand.

I return his embrace, wishing I could melt into him and make us one. I don't know anything about his father, but if I had to guess, he must have had something to do with the scars on Obsidian's back.

The man in my arms may have his issues, but I know without a doubt he would never, never do that to someone else, especially his own flesh and blood.

Tears prick my eyes as we draw apart, and Obsidian's large hands come to rest on my cheeks. "I need you, Ariana. Can I have you?"

He's come to me many nights while I've been sleeping, but without him saying it, I know this is different, even if I can't explain how.

"Yes." I nod. "Yes, you can always have me."

Sliding his hands under my knees and my back, he lifts us up and walks across the room and down the stairs. When he reaches his bedroom, he gently sets me on his mattress. Then he strips off his lounge pants before crawling across the mattress, hovering over me.

His twin pools-of-midnight eyes soak me in as he straightens, his palms sliding under the hem of my T-shirt, lifting it up my body and over my head. His face dips, and his tongue grazes my nipple, spurring it to a sharp point before repeating the pattern on my other breast. My hands dive into his wavy hair as he lowers himself and proceeds to kiss and suck every inch of my exposed skin. The fact that the only light comes from the sconces in the hallway because the door is open adds to the sensual feel.

Gripping one breast in his hand, he sucks on my nipple until I'm throbbing between my thighs, desperate for him. Eventually, he trails his tongue up to my collarbone and runs it along the column of my neck.

He whispers in my ear, "I want to deserve you. I want to be good to you. I really do."

As if my heart is made of glass, it shatters at his confession, at the sincerity and desperation and pain laced in the words. What has happened to this man that he believes he can't be that man for me?

I force him away from my neck so he can see my face when I say, "You do. You are."

He stares into my eyes as if he's willing himself to believe my words. His gaze slips to my mouth, and tension fills every inch of his bedroom. I want to wrap my hand around the back of his head and bring his mouth to mine, but this has to be his decision. He's the one who put that restriction on us, but as I lie with the weight of him over me, I wish and dream to know what his lips feel on mine. If it's even just for tonight.

"Fuck it," he says, his mouth crashing to mine.

My arms wrap around his shoulders, pulling him down on top of me, wanting all of him. His hard body falls on my soft one, crushing my breasts, and it's glorious. For the first time, his lips are on mine. And with this one single kiss, the small distance we were keeping from each other is obliterated.

We sink into the kiss, our tongues lazily lashing until I cede control.

I've never been kissed like this—as if he might die if he has to strip his lips off mine.

My hands skate over his back, the rough terrain of his scar tissue under my fingertips, as if I could magically heal them, heal him. Liquid fire damps between my legs, soaking my panties as I grind against his hard length rubbing against me. I need him inside me like I need my next breath.

Just when I think he's at the breaking point too, his lips leave mine, and I groan. Until his lips trail a path down my abdomen to the top of my pussy. He hooks his fingers under each side of my panties, sliding them down my legs before tossing them near my T-shirt.

His eyes remain on me as his mouth inches lower and lower until he's nestled between my legs. Slowly, with intention and absolute focus, he devours me with his tongue. His large hands splay my legs open while he sucks on my swollen nub, over and over, ratcheting up my desire one level at a time.

He doesn't increase the pace or change his tactics, and he stares at me through his long dark eyelashes, enjoying my rising pleasure. He takes me from a slow burn to a raging fire that overtakes me. My back arches off the bed, and my body stiffens.

"Obsidian," I plead, explosions bursting behind my closed eyelids.

He never takes his mouth off me, but slows, allowing me to enjoy the fall down.

I tug at his arms, needing him inside me. He comes willingly, his weight pushing down on me in the most delicious way, and his lips fall to mine again. I taste myself on his tongue and lips. We keep kissing, almost as though we've discovered this new facet between us, and we'll never tire of it. I know I won't.

My hands push into his hair, and he tugs on my bottom lip before sucking it into his mouth. My core tightens, wanting him to claim me in more ways than physically.

He pulls away and looks into my face. He slowly pushes into me, our gazes locked, and again, something shifts. Something different. I'm too invested to think of the repercussions. Even if I only have this Obsidian for tonight, I'll take it.

CHAPTER

TWENTY-SIX

I sink into Ariana, and she's still everything I desire.

I've been inside her many times, but this is different. Hell, I kissed her. Broke my rules about keeping her at arm's length, but I couldn't hold myself back. I wanted that intimacy, to feel the love and adoration only she offers me. And now that I know what sex feels like when it's about more than just getting off, I'll never have the strength to give her up, even if it's what's best for her.

With our bodies joined, my eyes don't stray from hers. She's the most beautiful woman I've ever seen. The only woman who, despite not knowing all the facets of my past, has seen who I really am beneath the veneer and still accepted me. The strongest woman I've known. The funniest, too. Everything about her is what I never knew I wanted and needed. What I've been missing.

She's a miracle come to life.

If I had a genie, I'd use all three wishes to be the man she deserves.

To be the man she needs me to be. Not like my father, a man who destroyed every good and precious thing he touched.

Our pleasure builds slowly, matching the emotion in my chest until tears glimmer in her eyes. When the first tear slides from the corner of Ariana's eye, I follow its path with my tongue, vowing to always be the one to soak up her tears and never cause them.

Love is a foreign concept to me when it comes to a woman. I've never made love to a woman, never even come close, but that's what we're doing. Just as I now know what it is to value someone else's happiness and needs over my own. My chest cracks open, and Ariana nuzzles her way in. Hell, she's been inching in since the day she showed up here.

"I love you, Ariana. So much that it hurts. So much that now that I've discovered this euphoria, I'm crippled by the knowledge I could fuck up and lose it." The words I've never said to anyone in my life slip free.

She brings her hands to my face, tracing her fingertips over my features while I rock into her. Then her hands slide to my back and crest over the physical scars that hold nothing to the emotional ones I've buried deep into my soul.

I've always been self-conscious of my scars, but when she brought her lips to the first one then kissed each one in turn, she released the pain those memories held. The shame that was present the first time someone discovered them drifted off into the ether.

"I love you too," she whispers, tears spilling. She's just as overcome with emotion as I am.

I bring my lips to hers, increasing the pace of my thrusts and driving us toward bliss and what feels like freedom.

A few minutes later, as if divined by the universe itself, we come at the same time, lips pressed together, wrapped in each other's arms, two hearts open and full of love. As I fall down on her body, hearing her labored breaths in my ear, I realize how badly I've fucked myself because she's ruined me. No one will ever compare to her.

I soften inside her, so I roll onto my back, tugging her with me so she's half lying on my chest, not willing to let her go yet.

Her leg drapes over me, and her fingertip runs a lazy path over my chest. "So much for sex only, huh?"

With the arm wrapped around her, I squeeze her and kiss the top of her head.

Hearing the words I love you did something to me. Rather than wanting to hide my shame in the dark, it's time to bring it into the light. What she's done for me, she deserves the truth.

"The first time my father burned me with one of his cigars was shortly after my mother died." Her finger stills on the path she's drawing, and I bring my hand over hers, squeezing it. "He was always a bastard, but things got worse after she died. She was the only good thing in this place. The only source of light."

"Obsidian, that's awful. My father isn't perfect by any

means, but what he did to you is unfathomable." Her voice holds the hurts, and I take comfort in her.

"Prior to that, he used to lock me in the closet in my room—not this one. I think that started around the time I was five or so. He'd lock me in there, and I'd beg and cry to be let out. It always felt like the walls were closing in on me. He'd leave me there so long I'd piss myself and have to sit in it for hours."

A shiver racks my spine when I remember the terror whenever he'd drag me toward that closet. I'd cry and sob for so long that by the time I was let out, I'd often lost my voice.

"I remember wondering what I'd done that was so bad to deserve it. Eventually I concluded that I must have been born with darkness inside me. A darkness my father recognized because it was in him too."

Ariana bolts up from my chest and stares at me with fire in her eyes. "That's not true."

I tuck a lock of her hair behind her ear, but I don't agree with her.

"It's not true, do you hear me? Stop thinking that about yourself." Tears well in her eyes, and I cup her face.

My sweet Ariana. What the hell did I ever do in this life to get her?

"He used to tell me all the time how much of himself he saw in me. How, out of all my brothers, I was the one he knew would grow up to be just like him. The idea of it terrified me. That's why..." I search her face. I don't want to cause her any more pain, but this feels like the moment to lay myself bare. "That's why I tried to end my life a decade ago."

She sucks in a breath, and something passes over her stricken expression I can't quite place. "Oh, Obsidian." The tears pooled in her eyes slip free. "Thank God you weren't successful."

"It had nothing to do with God. Kol found me and got my stomach pumped before it was too late."

"I don't care what your asshole of a father told you, you are not that man. You aren't filled with darkness. We all have pieces of ourselves that live in dark corners, but it doesn't make up the entirety of who you are. If it did, you wouldn't even care if you turned out like him."

She has a point. I've never thought about it that way.

I'm quiet, contemplating her words, when she says, "Can I ask you something?"

I trace my fingers over her forehead, down her temple, then along her jawline. "Anything."

"Why didn't your mom stop it from happening?"

It's a fair question. I'd ask her the same if the roles were reversed. "He was physically abusive toward her too. A lot of times, what my brothers and I were being punished for was sticking up for her and trying to intervene."

She shakes her head. "You were just children."

"That never mattered to him."

"How did your father die?"

I hold my breath, then it comes out as a rush of air. "That's the only thing I can't discuss with you, I'm sorry." I thread my hand through the hair at her temple.

She looks as though she wants to ask more, but respects what I said with a nod. "Well, however it was, I hope it was long and painful."

It was.

Ariana leans her head back down on my chest. "Thank you for telling me all of this. I know it must be difficult."

My hand runs up and down her side, basking in the feel of her soft skin. "I want you to know all of me, Ariana. I want to be worthy of your love."

She pops up again, this time straddling my lap and leaning in so we're surrounded by the flames of her red hair, noses touching, breathing in each other. "You are more than worthy, Obsidian."

Then she slides her body down mine and takes me in her mouth, obliterating any thoughts of the past. By the time she's finished with me, it's hard not to believe I'm the luckiest bastard in the world.

CHAPTER
TWENTY-SEVEN

ARIANA

This week has been a blur, and I can hardly believe it's Saturday. Between the beginning tendrils of friendship with Anabelle, Rapsody, and Cinder, and having Obsidian tell me he loves me, I'm floating on a cloud.

The only shadow to be found was in his confession of the abuse his father inflicted on him. I can't believe men like his father actually exist. Thank God that man is already dead, or I might have tracked him down and murdered him myself.

The day after Obsidian and I made love, I googled his father and found out that he was murdered just like his mother. The only difference is that Obsidian and his brothers were all suspects in his death at one point or another, but the police never had enough evidence, so the death remains unsolved.

Truth is, even if one of them did kill him, I'd be unbothered. Every monster deserves a monstrous death.

The driver stops the vehicle in front of Black Magic Bar, and I step out. My mood plummets when I stare at the door because I'm here empty-handed. I couldn't go through with stealing from the man I love. The moment Obsidian told me he loved me, it created a mountain of problems for me.

The guilt is so hard to wade through. Most of the time I can push it off, but if I happen to think about what I'm doing in his presence, I might burst out crying.

I had a small figurine in my hand earlier today, and I just couldn't leave the room with it. My feet were cement because even knowing I can never have Obsidian since he'll never forgive me, I still can't steal from him. And now I have to somehow tell my brother.

Pulling the door open, I step inside and find Bastion at his usual table. Once again, he's chatting with the bartender, but she leaves as she sees me approach.

He gets up from his seat and walks around the table to give me a hug. "How's it going, sis?"

I return his hug then sit. "It's going. You?"

He leans back in the chair, stretching one arm out in front of him on the table. "My sugar mama broke up with me."

"Let me guess, you're heartbroken?" I roll my eyes.

He chuckles. "No, but I do miss the influx of cash. And the sex was good."

I stick my finger in my mouth and gag. "Please don't share any details. What happened?"

Bastion shrugs. "Figured out I sold the watch she got me."

I cringe. "That'll do it."

"Yeah…" He sighs as the bartender returns, setting a beer down in front of each of us.

I nod toward her retreating back. "I bet you could solve the sex portion of your issue tonight."

His eyes watch her go back to the bar. "Yeah, if I had time, but I gotta visit your ass then jump on the red-eye home. Maybe she'll take pity on me and let me fuck her in the back before I leave."

"And they say romance is dead." I bring the beer to my lips.

"Do they?" He winks and takes a pull from his own.

"How's Dad?" Just like every week, I brace myself for whatever my brother is about to say.

"Managing to stay out of trouble." His gaze flicks from the beer in his hand up to me and back.

Something is off, and it's not his sugar mama breakup. He's not telling me something. "What?"

"What what?"

My head tilts. "Stop messing around. What is it? There's something you're not telling me."

He frowns. "Uma's not happy."

My heartbeat picks up speed. "Why isn't she happy? We've been paying off Dad's debt faster than she thought possible."

"I think that might be the problem." My forehead creases, and he continues. "She didn't say anything the first time I gave her a large sum of money, but every week when I'm there, she seems more put out. She's started asking how we're getting all this money and why I'm the one delivering it and not you. I think she has a real hard-on for you."

I think back to her comments about how she could use someone like me working for her. How together, we could do big things. My hand tightens around my beer. "You didn't tell her, did you?"

He shakes his head. "Hell no. The last thing we need is her sniffing around here and ruining a good thing."

"Agreed." My lips press into a thin line as suspicion rears its head. "Did she say anything else about me? Ask anything about me?"

He shakes his head. "No, she just wanted to know why you hadn't been back and where the money came from. When I wouldn't tell her, she dropped it. But I have a feeling it's going to come up again."

I lean over the table. "Whatever you do, do not tell her where I am. I don't want that viper anywhere near here."

Bastion scoffs at me. "As if." He lifts the beer to his lips.

I take a hefty pull off my beer.

"So, how's life working for the other half?"

"It's not so bad." My mind drifts to Obsidian and the vision of him naked in bed where I left him a short while ago. Hopefully he's still there when I return.

"What's that smile about?"

"What smile?"

"You just had this goofy smile on your face."

"I did not." I lift my beer to my lips.

"You did. What were you thinking about?"

"Nothing. Enough with the interrogation." I scowl at him.

Bast sets his beer on the table with force and sets his hands on the edge of the table. "You know, I thought something was up weeks ago, but now, I'm positive."

I shake my head. "I'm not going to listen to this." Standing, I grab my bag off the back of the chair and walk toward the door.

I'm only ten steps outside when Bastion flies out of the bar and brings me to a halt with a hand on my elbow. "What the fuck is going on, Ari?"

I'm cornered. There's no way to do what I feel is right in my heart and help my family.

Tears gather in my eyes, and I shake my head. "I can't."

"Tell me." He sets his hands on my shoulders and brings his face down to meet my eyes. "Are you sleeping with him?"

"Worse," I whisper, not wanting to tell my brother. I've broken every rule my dad has set when we go after a mark.

His hands fall to his sides, and he steps back then pushes them through his strawberry-blond hair. "You can't love him?"

I sniffle and nod. "And he loves me."

Bastion shakes his head. "C'mon, Ari. Why would a man like Voss fall in love with you? No disrespect, but the guy is a billionaire. He could have anyone—models, movie stars, other billionaires."

My brother's comments crack me open. He's only repeating everything my subconscious has been telling me since Obsidian said the words.

"I don't know, but he does," I shout at him.

Bastion grips my arm and walks me down the stairs at the side of the porch, moving me into the parking lot away from the bar. "So what, you're going to ride off into the sunset as a billionaire's bride and leave Dad and I to suffer the consequences? I'm sure the billionaire can keep you safe, right? Why worry about us?"

I rip my arm from his hand. "I'm not the one who got us into this mess!" My finger stabs him in the chest. "And of course I'm not going to leave you two to deal with it on your own. I don't know what I'm going to do, though. I can't steal from him anymore, Bast."

His mouth drops open. "You didn't bring anything with you tonight?"

"No! I couldn't do it. I've betrayed his trust so many times already, and I can't do it anymore."

A tear drips down my cheek, and Bastion pulls me in for a hug. "Okay, okay." He's quiet while he comforts me. "We're so close, Ari. With another couple of decent lifts from you, we have it paid off."

I shake my head into his chest, knowing I can't do it

anymore, then I step back, wiping the tears from my face with my hands. "We need to figure something else out."

He places his hands on his hips and looks at the ground. Then his head whips up. "If this guy loves you, could you just ask him for the money?"

"Bast, no! It would raise too many questions. I can't admit to him what I've already done, how I was raised, and who I used to be." The idea of Obsidian knowing that information about me spurs nausea as if I'm abandoned at sea on an innertube.

He blows out a breath. "I don't know what we're going to do then."

"Did your sugar mama give you anything else you can sell?"

Bastion shakes his head.

"Well, find another one then. Fast."

He nods.

"I'll see if I can think of something one of us can do," I add. We've spent a lot of my paycheck on Bastion flying back and forth every week. No matter, it's not going to cover a fraction of what we owe.

His disappointment is obvious, but he doesn't say anything further.

"I have to travel with Obsidian for work again this coming week, so I won't be able to meet you next Saturday." It's a lie. This Saturday is another Ritual Room meeting, but I can't tell him that.

God, I feel as if I'm lying to everyone I love, and I hate it.

Bastion eyes me suspiciously but accepts my excuse. "Fine, I'll see you in two weeks."

"Okay, take care of yourself." I give him another hug.

"Be careful, Ari. Remember, those people aren't like us." He squeezes me before letting go.

I used to think that, believed my dad when he told us that. But now I realize they're just as broken as the rest of us.

TWENTY-EIGHT

ARIANA

It's the night of the Ritual Room, and I'm way less nervous than the first time I walked down these stairs. The theme for tonight is Secret Agent Affair. Obsidian is dressed in a classic tuxedo and looks as devilishly handsome as ever. I'm wearing my hair down off to one side in a Hollywood wave and an off-the-shoulder teal gown with a sweetheart neckline. The dress is adorned with sequins that increase the farther down on the dress you go, and I feel like a princess.

Well, a naughty princess once Obsidian passed over the gold mask I was to wear. It even has snakes woven throughout. When I asked him why my mask wasn't black or red or white like everyone else there, he explained that the colors have significance. White is for people who just want to watch and not partake in any activities themselves. Black is for people who are down for anything—they don't need to give consent for each and every act.

The mask itself is the consent. And the red is for people in the middle who want to participate but want to know what they're getting into and then give their consent. According to him, I only need a gold mask because none of the other colors matter since I'm his. And I agree, he's mine.

He holds my hand and helps me down the steps that lead to the Ritual Room. My dress goes to my ankles tonight, so navigating the old stairs is tricky.

When I pictured what outfit Obsidian might want to put me in tonight, I pictured something risqué, so I was surprised when he brought this dress to my room. He'd just leaned in, kissed my neck, and told me that sometimes the hottest thing a woman could do was leave things to the imagination.

I smile as he leads me by the hand down the hall and into the main room. It's bustling with people, some with drinks in their hands. If it weren't for the masks, it would look like any other high-end party.

"What do we do now?" I lean into Obsidian's side.

"Mingle. Chat. Whatever we want, really."

The innuendo in his words makes my nipples pebble beneath my gown.

"Sid."

His name being called has us turning to see who it is. I know immediately that it's one of his brothers based on the mask he's wearing. It's like Obsidian's—gold—except this one is a lion. I remember what he told me about the tattoos and surmise that this is Rapsody's husband, Kol.

"Hey." Obsidian shakes his brother's hand with a smile. "Kol, I want you to meet Ariana."

Kol turns to me, and I see the makings of a small smile on his face. "It's good to finally meet you. You can't let this one hide you all the time."

"I'm equally to blame." I smile. "It's good to meet you. I had the pleasure of spending some time with your wife. She's wonderful."

His smile grows and jealousy kicks in with the thought of having Obsidian look like that when someone mentions me. "She is."

"Where is Rapsody?" Obsidian asks.

He looks over his shoulder. "Last I saw, she and Anabelle were gabbing about something in the corner." Kol turns back to look at me. "So how are you managing to put up with this one?" He motions to Obsidian with the hand holding his drink.

I lean into Obsidian and place my hand on his chest. "Aw, he's more bark than bite."

Kol chuckles. "With you maybe."

Another man approaches the group, and I figure it's Nero since he also has a gold mask on, this one a raven, and Cinder is by his side.

"I finally get to meet the woman who stole your heart," he says to Obsidian and clasps him on the shoulder before looking at me. "You're a miracle worker."

I feel my face heat beneath my mask. "I don't know about that."

"Trust me," he says. "I'm Nero, good to meet you."

"Nice to meet you, Nero."

"Leave them alone," Cinder says to him good-naturedly and rolls her eyes.

I make my way over to her, and the two of us chat for a bit. She tells me about the dance studio she runs in Magnolia Bend, just down the street from Black Magic Bar, and invites me to take one of her pole dancing lessons that she teaches one night a week.

"I'm not really that coordinated," I say with a laugh, thinking of my dance with Brandon in Washington, DC, where I stepped all over his toes for the first minute. I push that vile man from my thoughts.

"You don't need to be. It's hard work, but it just takes practice and building up your strength, I swear."

"Okay, I'll think about it."

Her words make me think about how I won't be here forever. How all of this will come to an end soon. I want to weep because I've never felt what I do here, but now isn't the time to dwell on it, especially since I got myself in this position.

Eventually, Obsidian slides his hand around my waist from behind, inching his hand lower, but just shy of where I really want him. He bends his head to say in my ear, "Do you want to leave this room?"

Cinder sees what's happening and politely excuses herself, unbothered by the interruption. I guess she's used to it.

I turn around to face him, wrapping my arms around his neck. "What did you have in mind?"

He places a chaste kiss on my lips. "I thought we could go into one of the other rooms and watch another couple play. See what happens."

I pull back a bit to meet his gaze. "You don't want us to…"

"Join them?" He glares at me. "Hell no. You're all mine. I have no intentions of sharing you. That's Nero's thing."

My mouth falls open. "He and Cinder… do that?"

Obsidian throws his head back and laughs. He looks glorious doing it. I know I'm not the only one who thinks so when a bunch of people turn around and take notice.

"Don't look so scandalized. You're standing in a sex club."

"I suppose." A grin forms on my face. "All right then. Lead the way."

He leads me by the hand down the hall to the row of doors. Some are open and some are closed, but he seems to know exactly which one to go to. Right before we go in, he turns and says to me over the music, "Daria and Kevin always like to put on a show."

We walk inside, and it's almost like a home theater. Stairs on either side of the room lead down to a stage where there's a large bed and some BDSM equipment. Each level is rather large, and some have couches, some chaise lounges, and some chairs.

Obsidian goes down three levels and has us sit side by side on one of the chaise lounges. There's a smattering of other people, but none of them are on the same level we are.

A naked couple walks out onto the stage. The woman wears a black mask, as does the man. Her brown hair flows down to her modest breasts, while he's lean and fit and blond.

At first, it's weird watching them when they come together for a kiss and he palms her breast, tweaking her nipple, but the uncomfortableness only lasts for a minute or two. By the time he has her on her knees in front of him with his fist in her hair, his dick sliding in and out of her mouth, my initial discomfort is forgotten.

I shift in my seat as my desire increases, and my clit swells. A quick glance at Obsidian's lap shows he's also turned on.

The man on stage pulls the woman's mouth off of him and makes her stand at the end of the bed with her hands on one of the end boards, bent over so she's exposed to us. Then he drops to his knees behind her and brings his face between her legs.

My nipples grow taut, and I resist the urge to tug on them. I imagine what that woman on stage is feeling, knowing how amazing it is when Obsidian does that to me. When she moans, I clamp my thighs together and quickly glance around the room. People have already begun having their own fun, while others silently watch.

I reach beside me and rub Obsidian's hard cock through his tuxedo pants. A small groan leaves my lips, imagining the weight of him in my hand, my mouth, and my pussy. He leans back and lets me feel him, his eyes hooded with lust.

The man on the stage continues his assault until the woman is writhing, pushing back onto his face, and comes on a loud cry. Satisfaction gleams in his gaze when he stands and walks over to a small dresser, then pulls out something. I realize it's lube when he squirts some down the crack of her ass and rubs it along his long, thick shaft. He pushes one of her ass cheeks to the side, then slowly guides his cock into her ass with the other.

My insides clench. I've never done that, but it's something I wouldn't mind trying with Obsidian. I squeeze his dick harder.

His fingers manipulate his belt and lower his zipper, pulling out his straining cock. "Come here. I want to fuck your cunt while we watch."

He drags me onto his lap, guiding me to face the stage so that my back is to his front. It feels so good to finally have his hands on me, even if it is only my arms. He releases me too soon, but then I realize he's working his way through the skirts of my dress, making it so my core is exposed to his cock, and I relax.

The moment his bare cock brushes against my folds, a long and satisfying moan slips free. The tip of his dick pierces my opening as he lines it up with my entrance. His one hand lands on my hip, his fingers flexed on my waist, lowering me to sink down.

His hot breath hits my ear when he whispers, "Now get yourself off however you want to."

I move and look up to find another man has joined the couple on stage. He's naked too, and he stands in front of the woman between her and the footboard. She takes his erection in hand and brings it to her mouth.

I rock up and down on Obsidian's dick, and when I look over my shoulder, I see that he's watching the show onstage as well. His hands move to my hips, and he squeezes, but he stretches his fingers open as if he's trying to stop himself from taking control.

The feeling of him stretching me is divine, and I melt into a steady rhythm while the people on stage continue, seemingly unaware of the audience. Looking around, I see a woman down a few rows from us on her knees in front of a man, and on the level below us, I see two women kissing and fondling each other.

My lust ignites to a level I didn't expect, and I speed up my pace as my breasts grow heavy. Obsidian's hands come to my waist, unable to stop himself, and he forcefully slams me down on his lap several times. He's so deep that it borders on painful, but it turns me on.

There's something erotic as hell about getting fucked so publicly. Everyone knows what we're doing, but no one can see anything other than Obsidian dressed in his tux with me in my dress on his lap.

One of his hands snakes under the layers of fabric of my dress, and his fingers find my swollen and needy clit. I suck in a breath—it feels as if all the air has been stolen from my lungs. My body draws tight, and my walls contract around him as he stretches me and delves in and out.

I gasp at the look of rapture on the face of the man getting the blowjob, and when the woman cries out and convulses as she comes, I come too, slamming down on Obsidian's lap and holding myself, gyrating my hips until his cock swells and jerks inside me. He comes so hard, his hand on my waist squeezes painfully.

He nuzzles his head into my neck from behind. "Fuck, woman. I'm never gonna get enough of you."

I wind my arm around his head, into the hair at the back of his head. "I know what you mean."

And that's what scares me the most. The words us and forever will never belong in the same sentence.

CHAPTER

TWENTY-NINE

OBSIDIAN

The day after our second Ritual Room visit, I surprise Ariana by whisking her away on my private plane to my home in the Bahamas.

I've always liked having money, sure, but since she came into my life, I've appreciated it on a different level. I want to give her everything. I've traveled quite a bit for Voss Enterprises, and I've traveled for pleasure, but now I want to travel with someone. I want to show her everywhere around the world she's never had the opportunity to go. I want to make love to her on every continent, in every hemisphere, in every time zone. Nothing is too good for my good girl.

"So, what do you think?" I ask as we step onto the balcony that overlooks the crystal-blue water and white sand beach.

"Obsidian, this is so beautiful. This is your home?"

I nod, wrapping my arm around Ariana's waist and pulling her into my side. "Yeah, I don't get here often. But we can change that if you want." I look down at her and swear I see a flash of sadness cross her face. I frown. "What's wrong?"

She shakes her head. "Nothing. You are absolutely perfect."

I give her a quick kiss, but it turns into something more before I force myself to pull away. "We should stop. The chef will be here shortly to make us dinner. Figured we could eat with this view tonight. Then tomorrow, I have a surprise."

She grins, her blue eyes lighting up. "I like surprises."

"Good. I think you're going to really like this one." I kiss the end of her nose.

"Will you give me a hint?"

I shake my head. "No way. You'll find out tomorrow."

She sinks to her knees in front of me, and her hands go for the button and zipper on my shorts. "What about now?"

I chuckle. "I just told you the chef will be here any minute. Maybe I'm right, and you are an exhibitionist."

"Let's test that theory, shall we?"

I'm about to pull her up when she palms my cock, brings my head to her lips, and does a thorough job of convincing me. I end up telling her the surprise in three minutes.

"I'M SO excited for this. Thank you!" She leans over the console and kisses my cheek.

When I told her last night that we were going to a nearby resort to swim with dolphins, I could tell she was ecstatic, but she had a mouth full of cock at the time, so expressing her excitement was difficult.

But even through breakfast this morning, it was clear she couldn't wait to get here.

"Have you ever done this before?" I pull up in front of the resort and park my car at the valet stand.

Ariana shakes her head. "No, my dad never really took us on vacations when I was growing up."

She never says much about her family. Sometimes I think it's because she's embarrassed that she didn't come from money, but other times, I can't help but wonder whether she's hiding something. Maybe something else she's embarrassed about.

There's no need for her to. I've already confessed to her how fucked up my family is.

I get out of the car, and the valet comes over to take the key. I wave off the other staff member who is about to open Ariana's door, then I help her out.

We make our way through the resort, one of the hotel managers leading the way because this place is huge and it would be easy to get turned around. When we get to the large pool, one of the trainers meets us there.

The first thing we have to do is change into wetsuits. Ariana removes the short sundress she's wearing, and I watch the trainer to make sure there's no interest in his eyes and that he's not leering at her in her bikini because, damn, does she look good. He's smart enough to divert his eyes until she has the body suit on.

Next, he explains how it will work and what the dolphins will do. Ariana is practically buzzing with excitement, and I rub her back while we listen to the instructions.

"Any questions?" the trainer asks, clapping his hands in front of himself.

"Nope!" Ariana says excitedly.

Each of us walks over to the edge of the pool, and she makes a perfect swan dive into the water.

Once I'm in and above the water, treading water beside her, I say, "That was quite the dive."

She smiles at me, but there's a glimmer of something in her eyes. "I was a lifeguard."

That explains her comfort in the water. I saw her in the pool that one time at the manor, but it wasn't long enough to get a sense for how good of a swimmer she is.

The entire time we're in the pool with the dolphins, Ariana is beaming. She hangs onto the dolphin's fin as it pulls her through the water, and her laughter rings out. At times I have to stop and watch her, wanting to commit the moment to memory for the times when I'm feeling low and doubting whether or not I can make her happy.

Our time ends too soon, and she's reluctant to leave the water. It's as though she finds the same peace here as I do with her. But we do get out of the pool and return the wetsuits, thanking the trainer for his assistance.

On the walk back to the car, I interlace our fingers, and Ariana pulls me to a stop.

"Thank you so much for arranging this, Obsidian. It's one of the most special things I've ever done."

I kiss her. "I just want to see you happy."

Her hand cups my cheek. "I'm happier than I've ever been in my entire life. Never doubt that I love you."

"I love you more." My hand goes in her hair, and I kiss her again, probably with a little more vigor than I should in public, but I don't give a fuck.

When we break the kiss, she says, "Not possible."

THE NEXT MORNING, we take a Jeep around the island to explore and visit some local markets and the rum cake factory. In the afternoon, I take her to swim with the pigs, and as expected, she loves it. That night, we bathe together in the oversized tub and make love on the balcony of the master suite, overlooking the ocean.

On our final day, we go snorkeling. I'm once again amazed by how proficient she is in the water. She's like a fucking mermaid, diving down deep to see the fish and holding her breath for way longer than I can.

Everything about our time on the island has been perfect, and I despise that we have to return to Midnight Manor. But I can't afford to be away from work any longer than I already have been, especially since I planned this trip last minute.

As she takes her seat beside me on the private plane, I take note of the smattering of freckles on her face. They're more pronounced after days spent in the sun and make her look younger, closer to her twenty-four years.

She takes my hand. "This entire trip has been like a whole new world for me. Thank you for bringing me here, Obsidian. I can't remember a time I had so much fun and felt so relaxed."

Squeezing her hand, I kiss her temple. "I'm glad you enjoyed yourself. I'm only sorry we couldn't stay longer."

She frowns, and it feels as if there's more behind it than just being disappointed the fun has to end. "Yeah, back to reality."

"Don't worry, this won't be the last time we're here. I plan on us visiting this place many, many times together."

Tears glisten in her eyes as she takes me in.

I frown because there's something she's not telling me. "What's wrong?"

She shakes her head and sniffles. "Nothing. I'm just so happy. I never even knew I could be this happy."

I feel the same. I am so fucking thankful this woman came into my life. Still, I can't get rid of the sense that the clock is ticking on our time together. I tell myself the dread I feel is just my paranoia over losing the best thing in my life because everything good has always been taken away from me.

Maybe that's what love means—you search and search for it, then after you find it, all you do is worry about losing it.

CHAPTER

THIRTY

ARIANA

Since we returned from the Bahamas, Obsidian has insisted that I eat in the dining room with everyone else, which has been nice. It's allowed me to get to know his brothers a little better, but more than that, it's helped me form friendships with the ladies.

So I'm disappointed when they ask me if I'd like to have a girls' night on Saturday, and I have to put them off because I'm supposed to meet my brother. I'm meeting him even though I'll be showing up empty-handed again.

I haven't been able to think of anything we can do to pay off the remaining part of the loan, but I'm hopeful that my brother will have figured something out. Though I look forward to seeing Bastion, I hate the reason we're getting together.

The weight of my guilt is dragging me down like cement shoes pulling me to the bottom of the dark ocean. I'm thinking about that guilt when Obsidian's voice pulls me from my thoughts.

"Maybe one of these weeks I can tag along? I'd love to meet your brother under better circumstances." He arches an eyebrow.

I try to keep a natural smile on my face when I answer. "Of course. But he doesn't know anything about us yet... I'm not sure how he'll feel about it, since you're my boss and all."

Obsidian frowns, but nods in understanding. I hate this.

"You know how it is... big brothers can be overbearing at times. Give me some time to ease him into the idea of us."

He pulls me into him and places a chaste kiss on my lips. "Makes sense. You let me know when you think it's a good time for us to meet. I want to make a better impression than I did."

His words, as well as the heartfelt emotion behind them, make my chest ache. I hate that Obsidian still questions whether he's good enough for me, when I'm the liar and the cheat.

We say our goodbyes, and I promise to come find him when I return later. The manor feels darker and more ominous than usual as I walk toward the front door to meet the driver. I have no doubt it's probably my subconscious making me feel that way. Though this place is creepy as hell sometimes.

I'm dropped off in front of Black Magic Bar as usual, but when I go inside, I don't find Bastion waiting for me at our usual table. Figuring he's probably running late, I walk over to the bar and order myself a beer, then sit at our usual table to wait.

By the time I'm halfway through my beer, worry sets in. He's never been late before. Maybe there was an issue with his flight? The weather is fine here, but maybe there are storms on the West Coast.

I didn't have time to go to my room and check the phone I use to communicate with him. Maybe he sent me a message to say that he couldn't come.

Once I'm finished with my beer, I decide to wait another half hour before I text the driver to pick me up. But a half hour later, he still hasn't shown.

Before I leave, I go back up to the bar to speak with the bartender. "Hey, you didn't see my brother at all tonight, did you?"

She smiles at me. "That handsome guy who always flirts?"

I return her smile, though it's forced. "That's the one."

She shakes her head. "No, he hasn't been in here."

My muscles grow a little more tense. "If he does come in, can you please tell him to text me?"

"Sure thing. Everything okay?" She tilts her head.

"I'm sure it's fine." I give her my thanks and walk outside to meet the driver.

As soon as I get back to Midnight Manor, rather than going straight to Obsidian's room, I head to my bedroom to pull out the phone I hide there. When I pull it out from under the mattress, I see that there's no message from Bastion, so I type one out to him.

EVERYTHING ALL RIGHT? Where were you tonight?

I WAIT a few minutes and don't receive a reply, so I slide it back under the mattress, tension lacing my body.

Where the hell is my brother?

By MONDAY MORNING, Bastion still hasn't returned my text, and I'm so worried that I make an excuse to leave Obsidian's office and sneak off to call my father, even though I'm still pissed at him. My heart goes into full panic when he doesn't answer either.

I return to Obsidian's office, not wanting to give him any cause for alarm. I stop in his doorway, seeing someone sitting across from him at his desk.

In the months I've worked here, I've never seen anyone else from the outside at the manor, let alone in Obsidian's office. She must be someone high up in Voss Enterprises, but Obsidian never said anything to me about a visitor today.

Obsidian looks away from the person and smiles, but there's a tension to his face I haven't seen in weeks. "Ariana, I'd like you to meet someone. This is Leah."

With a smile, I walk around to the side of the desk and turn to greet the woman but freeze when I see who sits in the chair.

Uma.

Air whooshes from my lungs in a rush, and my right hand falls to the edge of the desk to stay upright. She grins at me as though she gets pleasure from my reaction.

"Are you okay?" Obsidian says, rolling his chair closer to me.

I place my hand over my stomach because bile runs up my throat. I have no idea what's going on here, why she's here and calling herself Leah, but I know for certain it is not good. My heart pounds, and my pulse sounds like a freight train in my ears.

"Yes, sorry. I didn't eat enough at breakfast." Recovering enough to give her a smile, I say, "It's good to meet you, Leah."

Her hand rises, and I follow the movement to see her rub my necklace just as I always did. My mother's necklace, the one Uma made me give her for collateral, is snug on her neck and the bile sours, making me cough.

"Leah, this is my assistant, Ariana."

"Wonderful to meet you, Ariana. I'm sure you must count yourself lucky to be working for a man like Mr. Voss."

She knows.

My hands form fists at my sides, but I attempt to keep my voice casual. "I'm very lucky indeed."

Is that why she's here? To blow my cover and rat me out to Obsidian? Or just to make me sweat?

I turn to Obsidian. "How do you know Leah?"

He shifts in his seat. "We met briefly when I was on the West Coast a few months ago."

Wait—what?

My heart riots. I need to sit down. "Well, it was good to meet you, Leah. I'll leave you both to it." I walk on wooden legs over to my desk and sit, taking a moment to gather myself.

I need to contact Bastion and find out what the hell is going on, but the phone I use to communicate with him is hidden in my bedroom.

So instead, I pretend to work, catching snippets of their conversation. I can't hear much, but Uma laughs as though whatever Obsidian says is the most humorous thing she's ever heard.

Eventually he picks up the phone on his desk, and I hear him say, "Marcel, we're going to have a new guest staying with us for a while. Please have one of the rooms in my wing set up."

I blanch and try not to show my reaction, my fingers typing gibberish in a Word doc. She's going to stay here? Jesus, this is so much worse than I thought.

They talk for another couple minutes, then Obsidian stands and sees her to the door of his office.

"Bye, Ariana. It was great to meet you," she says as she

strides confidently across the room, waving and never giving away that we know one another.

I turn in my chair and give her a small smile, then face my computer again. When I hear the office door close, I finally turn to face Obsidian, trying to school my features. "She's staying here?"

He walks over and takes my hands, pulling me up out of my chair and into an embrace. "It's not like that."

"What is it like then?"

He pulls back and looks at me with something akin to amusement. "I like this jealous side of you."

In an attempt to calm my racing heart, I draw in a deep breath. "Who is she, Obsidian?" I need to figure out how they know each other before I blurt my entire truth to him.

His lips dip. Then he tugs me by the hand over to the sitting area, takes a seat on the couch, and pulls me into his lap. I brace myself for him to tell me she's his former lover or something.

"Before we met... I was so fucked up. My head was a mess. You know very well the issues I have."

Despite the dire situation, my heart squeezes, and I place a hand on his cheek. "We've talked about this."

"I know." He kisses my palm. "But back then, all my brothers had just found love themselves, and I didn't see where I fit. Didn't feel loveable." He presses his face into my neck. "You're the only one who's ever made me feel differently, made me see *myself* differently." He pulls back and tucks my hair behind my ear.

"I feel the same way, Obsidian."

He gives me a sad sort of smile. "I know." He sighs. "I was staying by the ocean, and a storm rolled in. I'd been learning to surf for a couple weeks and wasn't half bad, I suppose, but that particular day, I was feeling forlorn, and I risked my life by going out into the ocean to try to surf during the storm."

Tears prick my eyes as I look at him and ask the question I've been wondering since the day I pulled him out of that water. "Did you do it because you knew it would end your life?"

He shakes his head. "I honestly don't know. Ten years ago… that was an explicit attempt. This was more… let fate decide."

I frown, his face becoming blurry as the unshed tears in my eyes thicken.

"Long story short, I went under and would have drowned if someone hadn't pulled me from the water and given me CPR. I tried to find out who saved me, but she took off right after. I even had an investigator try to find her for me."

"What does that have to do with Leah?"

"She's her." He kisses the hollow of my neck.

"You think Leah is the one who saved you?" I bite my cheek to prevent the truth from escaping.

"I know she is. All I could remember was a voice, a melody and one other thing. A necklace. Did you see the one she was wearing?"

I stiffen at the mention of my mother's necklace, but Obsidian doesn't seem to notice. "Yes, it was quite nice."

"I remember that locket and the pearls hanging in front of me. That's how I know it was her."

"What does she want?"

His forehead creases. "What do you mean?"

My head tilts. "You're a billionaire. She must be here because she wants something. Has she told you what it is?"

His hand rubs my hip then squeezes. "She just recently went back to the beach. She was so shaken up over what happened it took her that long to want to go in the water again. Someone there mentioned how a guy I'd hired had been asking around about who saved me, so she called me, and I asked her to come here. She hasn't asked for money, but I'm going to offer her some in the hopes that she'll take it."

My hand runs down his shoulder, and my fingers flex, grabbing his shirt for a second before I smooth the fabric back out. "You can't do that."

My reaction must come across with the panic I feel because he looks at me strangely and removes my hand from his shirt. "Why not?"

Because once Uma knows she can get money out of you, she'll never stop trying to siphon you dry. She'll never go away and leave us alone.

I shrug, trying to temper my reaction. "I just think it sets a dangerous precedent. What if she comes back for more?"

Obsidian slides his hand into the hair at the back of my head and draws my face forward. "I owe her. If it weren't for my accident, my brothers likely never would have hired me an assistant, and I never would have met you. I have her to thank for saving me and setting me on this new course in my life—you."

He's not wrong, only he doesn't know the twisted truth behind his words.

"I heard you tell Marcel to make up a room for her. Why is she staying here?"

"She didn't make any arrangements for herself before she came into town. She's between jobs at the moment, so I told her she can stay as long as she likes." He shrugs as though it's no big deal. "I owe her everything I have, Ariana."

I nod and place a chaste kiss on his mouth. "Okay, I just wasn't sure what was going on. Sorry if I came on strong."

He grins. "No apology necessary. Be jealous anytime." He gives me a kiss that leaves little doubt as to whether I should be concerned that Leah's caught his eye or not.

But that's not what I'm worried about at all. I want to know the real reason Leah's here.

THAT NIGHT, I tell Obsidian I'm not feeling well and that I'm going to sleep in my own bed.

I'm awoken in the middle of the night by him pushing into me from above. I don't know how I never hear him open the heavy bedroom door that creaks on its hinges. It takes me a moment to get my bearings, as it always does, but the delicious stretch around his girth makes me hum in approval.

I forget that a snake is sleeping under the same roof as us. Then again, maybe I'm the snake.

We never speak when he comes to me like this. At least nothing more than the soft, murmured words of desperation when we're close to climaxing.

He rocks into me, black eyes glittering down at me with so much love and adoration that it makes me want to weep. This may be the last time we get to experience something like this together. I've betrayed him, and I have no doubt that he's close to finding out. He'll know what a liar I am and how I'm the one who's not good enough for him.

My hands go into his hair, and he bends down and kisses me. Our mouths part, and our tongues meet, slowly circling in a dance of their own.

My orgasm builds inside me, and when my walls clamp down around him, he spills into me, and I will myself to commit this feeling to memory, wishing I could bottle it up like that jar of sand Obsidian has from the beach. So that I can always remember what it feels like to be loved by a man like Obsidian, because it's moments from ending, I know it.

THIRTY-ONE

OBSIDIAN

Ariana has been on edge for the past two nights. The first night Leah arrived, she got settled, but the next night, I insisted to Ariana that we dine with Leah out on one of the patios to show my appreciation. Ariana barely said a word the entire meal.

I'm not sure if it's jealousy making her act so out of character, but I don't think so. It seems like something more than that, something different, but I can't quite put my finger on it. When I questioned her after dinner, she said she was tired and still not feeling one hundred percent.

I'm on my way back to my office, one of Mrs. Potter's amazing cappuccinos in hand, when Marcel calls my name from behind me. I stop and turn to face him. His jaw is tense, and he's frowning.

"Everything okay, Marcel?"

"Sir, if I could have a word please. There's something I've wanted to talk to you about."

My forehead wrinkles, and I set the cappuccino on a nearby table before setting my hands on my hips. Marcel has been working for the Voss family as far back as I can remember. He's a loyal worker who knows how to keep his mouth shut, so the apparent concern on his face raises some red flags.

"What is it?" I ask.

He swallows hard and hesitates, almost as though he's considering how he wants to say what he has to say. The pause puts me on the edge.

"Spit it out," I snap.

He nods. "Sir, Finn came to me after some of the house-keeping staff went to him over the past several weeks with concerns. Apparently, they've noticed that items have gone missing from within the manor." He raises his chin and waits for my response.

"Items? What kind of items?"

"Candlesticks, a Fabergé egg, among other things."

A creeping feeling webs in my gut. "And why are you telling me specifically?"

He clears his throat. "Because, sir, the items didn't go missing until Miss Clarke came under your employment."

His words hang between us.

My immediate reaction is disbelief, but anger is quick to follow. "Are you accusing Ariana of stealing from us?"

Marcel's gaze darts away. "I'm just relaying the facts, sir."

I step toward him, but Marcel holds his ground. "How do you know it's not one of the housekeeping staff taking the items and using Ariana as a scapegoat because she's new on the premises?"

"I don't, sir. That's why I'm telling you. So you can tell me how you'd like me to proceed to figure out what's going on. Whether you want me to call the police."

"No police," I say.

"Very well. What would you like me to do?"

My mind races like a Formula 1 car in Monaco, every thought looping around to the same place—is this what's been bothering Ariana lately?

"I want you to keep this between the two of us. Leave it with me. I'll get to the bottom of it."

"Yes, sir." He gives me a small nod in deference before walking away.

I push a hand through my hair and blow out a breath. What the fuck is going on?

It can't be true. It can't.

But that oily feeling I've had a few times, like everything with Ariana is temporary, rises.

If Ariana was stealing things, when the hell would she have even had time to pawn them or find a buyer? She can't be hoarding them in her room. The housekeeping staff would have found them.

She never leaves the manor without me except... fuck. She meets her brother every Saturday night. I didn't think anything of it, but what brother comes to see his sister once a week? And where is he coming from? She's never given me the impression that he lives around here, and I've never bothered to ask.

I assume he lives wherever she lived before coming to Midnight Manor, but I don't know where that is. In the beginning, I refused to look at her employment file because I was planning to make her quit. After a while, I didn't want to know anything she didn't tell. Why didn't she tell me?

Tonight, I'll be paying a visit to Black Magic Bar.

I need to know for sure that everything Marcel is saying is bullshit, and I don't want the staff whispering about her in dark corners. I'll clear her name.

I STEP into Black Magic Bar, and there are only a few patrons. I sit at the opposite end of the bar from the old-timers but can tell they know who I am when they do a double-take and whisper to each other.

When the bartender is done helping them, she sidles down to me. "Can I get you something?"

I pull a one-hundred-dollar bill from my money clip and slide it across the bar top. "Just a water."

Her eyebrows rise, but she slides the bill into her back pocket. "Water it is." She fills one of the glasses with water and slides it over before coming to stand in front of me, leaning on the bar with her chin on her hand. "I'm assuming you're looking for a little more than just water."

Smart woman.

I pull my phone from my suit pocket and pull up a picture of Ariana from the Bahamas. Setting the phone on the bar, I turn it to face her and slide it closer. "Do you recognize this woman?"

Her gaze flits down to take a look. "Yeah, she's usually in here every Saturday. Don't know her name though."

"That's fine, I don't need it." I click the button on the side of my phone, making Ariana's picture disappear—which is for the best. I feel like the worst guy imaginable, doubting and questioning the woman I love. The only thing that could make it worse would be her face looking up at me while I did it.

"What do you want to know then?"

Someone else walks into the bar and sits at one of the tables, and she lifts her finger to tell them to give her a minute.

"Who's she usually here with?" I ask.

"Her brother. At least that's what they say. I think it's the truth, though, because he always flirts with me in front of her, and she never seems bothered by it."

I nod. "Anything stand out about their interactions?"

She presses her lips together and looks at the ceiling before flicking her gaze back to mine. "Not really. They both order beer, don't cause any trouble. Just sit at that table and talk for a while." She gestures at one of the tables.

I'm not sure whether I'm relieved or not. Her words haven't helped me get any closer to the truth.

"Okay, thanks for your help. I'll let you get back to work." I push up off the bar stool and stand.

"Oh, wait."

I still as dread crawls up my spine like a scorpion.

"There was this one time I was out back smoking a cigarette when they were leaving. He was parked at the back of the parking lot, so I could see them. She went to his car with him, which I thought was weird because I'd seen her get picked up by a driver the other times she'd been here."

My eyebrows raise to my hairline. "And..."

"She passed him something." She shrugs. "Not sure what exactly. Maybe drugs? I dunno, he just stashed it in his car really quick. Just the way they did it felt kind of shady to me, like a drug deal, you know? They didn't seem like druggies to me, but after I saw that, I wondered."

A pit forms in my stomach. Could Ariana have been passing her brother something she stole from the manor? Or am I blind to a drug problem?

"Thanks for the info." My voice is reed-thin, and I turn to exit the bar in a daze.

No, this can't be true. Ariana hasn't been playing me for months so she could steal from me.

But deep down, doubt rears its ugly head. I always felt Ariana would be taken from me, but maybe I had it reversed, and she's been *taking* from me.

CHAPTER

THIRTY-TWO

ARIANA

With Obsidian out of the house, I finally have the opportunity to confront Uma.

What game is she playing? During dinner last night, she was perfectly pleasant, giving no indication as to what or who she truly is. But I was nearly frozen in fear the whole time that she'd blurt out that she knew me, knew I'd been stealing from the Vosses. The entire dream of a life here with Obsidian will crumble.

I can't take the tension anymore.

Can't take the waiting for the ticking bomb to explode.

I'm going to have a nervous breakdown.

And so, I go in search of her and find her lounging in one of the many living areas in the east wing. She doesn't seem the least bit surprised to see me.

"Hello, Ariana, how are you this evening?"

"Cut the shit, Uma. What are you doing here?"

She grins like a tiger playing with a boar. I hate that she knows she has me. "What do you mean? You know why I'm here." She flicks her black hair off her shoulder and leans back in the seat, arms spread wide and looking for all the world as though she's as relaxed as can be.

I step closer to her. "I want to know why you're *really* here."

"I'm not going to tell you. Not yet anyway."

"Is this a game to you?" I raise my voice.

"Nothing about this is a game, Ariana, you know that. And if it were, I only play to win. Something to keep in mind."

My hands fist at my sides. God, I want to straddle her and strangle her, watching her take her last breath. "Isn't it enough that you're forcing my family to pay you so much money plus a ridiculous amount of interest? Now you're here to what, fuck with my life?"

Amusement glints in her eyes. "Maybe I'll just fuck Obsidian instead. I bet he's like a wolf in bed." She arches a dark eyebrow.

"Over my dead body."

Uma smirks. "Oh, really?"

"I don't know what the hell you're doing here, but you need to leave. Now. You'll get your money. This wasn't part of the deal."

She chuckles deep in her throat, but it lacks any humor. "Now, now, Ariana. What would Obsidian think if he heard you talking to me like this?" She clucks her tongue, and her hand covers my necklace around her neck. She rubs her finger and thumb around it. "The woman who saved his life."

Hearing her refer to him as Obsidian over and over grates on me. Almost everyone calls him Sid or Mr. Voss except me.

"If he knew who you really were and what you were capable of…"

"The same could be said of you." She narrows her eyes, her face hardening into her usual criminal killer one.

"I want you gone by the morning, or I'm telling him who you really are."

She shakes her head. "We both know you won't do that. Too much to lose. Guess you're stuck with me."

A frustrated scream releases from me, and I stomp across the massive room toward the exit. This got me nowhere. Now she knows she has me underfoot.

Racing out of the room into the hallway, I pull up short, finding Obsidian. His face is drained of color, and the love that is usually overflowing from his face is gone, replaced with horror.

"How much of that did you hear?" I whisper, tears welling.

He doesn't say a word before he gives me his back and stalks down the hallway. I race after him, almost having to run to keep pace.

"Obsidian, wait. Please." I grab hold of his suit jacket, but he yanks his arm out of my grasp.

Unshed tears burn my eyes as I follow him into his bedroom. Twenty paces in, he whips around to face me. Devastation is all I see reflected back, and I have never loathed myself more than in this moment.

"Let me explain," I beg, stepping closer, but he holds up his hand and steps back.

"I didn't catch much of your conversation, but enough to know that you and Leah know each other." He shakes his head as if he can't make the words make sense. "Enough to know that you've been lying to me!"

I cringe at the sound of his anger and disdain, yet I know I deserve it.

It was always going to come to this. I couldn't continue lying to him anyway.

Sucking in a deep breath, I decide to lay the truth all out there. At this point, it's over anyway, and he deserves to know that I'm the fucked-up one between us. "Her name is Uma."

He blinks several times as though he doesn't know what I'm saying, can't comprehend that Leah isn't Leah.

"She's not the one who saved you on that beach. I am."

His face pales, and he pushes a hand through his thick hair, tugging on the strands. "But the necklace..."

"It's my necklace. Correction. It was my mother's, and it's the only thing she left for me before she took off. I was forced to give it to Uma as collateral for a large debt my father owes her."

His face twists, and he doesn't say anything for a second. "You've been stealing from me to pay a debt?"

My throat squeezes painfully around the truth that tries to rise up out of it. I blink and a single tear topples down my cheek. "Yes," I whisper.

I don't know how he knows I've been stealing from him, but that's not my biggest worry at the moment.

"There's so much you don't know about me. That I haven't told you." I walk over to the sitting area, my legs unable to hold me up any longer. "My dad isn't a good guy. Not the worst kind of guy by any means, but my entire life, my dad has never had a real job. He's a grifter, always running some kind of scheme on someone."

Obsidian stands in front of where I'm sitting. I look away from him, not wanting to see the revulsion in his eyes.

"From the time I was little, he taught me how to run cons on people. When I was a kid, he used my youth and innocence against people's naiveté. When I was a teenager, he used my beauty against men's lust for the forbidden. The only reason I became a lifeguard after high school was because my dad wanted me to work at a country club so I could steal from the rich people or act as a honey trap." I shake my head, feeling disgust at myself for ever going along with any of my dad's plans. "Bast isn't even my real brother. My dad took him in when he ran away from home because even as a kid, Bast was good at hustling on the streets. That's my dad though. He's always been an opportunist."

"Why are you here?" His voice is hard, and I chance a glance up at him, finding the disgust I expected.

"My dad got mixed up with Uma and owed her a lot of money, an amount we couldn't have possibly paid off in the three months she demanded. After I saved you on the beach, I ran away because I was taught to never have anything to do with the cops. Even something good like saving a billionaire's life could mean a lot of media attention I didn't want and lead to people prying into my past. When I found out who I'd saved, my brother and dad wanted me to reach out and demand money from you." I shake my head. "It didn't feel right. Besides, I had no way to prove it was me."

Obsidian lets a sadistic chuckle loose. "That didn't feel right, but stealing from me does?"

"Of course not!" I plead with my eyes for him to believe me, but he shakes his head and looks at me like he did that first day I came to the manor. "I applied for the job, and when I got it, my brother and I planned that I would steal things, then pass them off to him to fence and get the money to Uma. At first, I told myself that you wouldn't even notice anything was gone, you have so much here, who was I really hurting? But as I got to know you... fell in love with you... I felt such guilt about it. I told Bast that I couldn't do it anymore." My head falls into my hands. "I know that doesn't make it okay."

Tears leak onto my palms, and I sob for a minute, but Obsidian remains quiet. When I finally raise my head and look at him, the rage lining his features frightens me.

"Was this all just some game, then? Keep me distracted so I wouldn't figure out what you were up to? Make me easy to deal with, pliable in case you were discovered? Maybe you hoped I'd never believe it if you were accused."

I bolt up off the couch. "No! My feelings for you are real. I love you!"

He sneers. "Enough with your lies. I can't even stomach looking at you." He prowls to the door and leaves without another word.

It feels as though he dropped the cracked heart I thought I was piecing back together in my lap.

CHAPTER
THIRTY-THREE

My chest has been hollowed out. Scraped clean from the inside.

I stalk from the room, unsure where I'm going, just knowing that I can't be in the same room as her any longer. Can't stand to look at the fucking liar.

When I think of all the things I shared with her, I want to be sick. She knows me in a way that no one else does and why? Because I believed every piece of bullshit that came out of her mouth. What a fool. I've always prided myself on not being able to be led around by the dick. Who knew I had to be worried about my heart?

I was fooled by a fucking con artist.

The shadows gather around me as I make my way through the manor and find myself in Kol's wing.

I'm so devastated and heartbroken, I don't know what to do with myself. Don't know what I'm even doing here. What the hell is Kol going to say that's going to make this better? Nothing can make this better.

"Kol!" I shout over and over as I walk aimlessly down the hallway, having no idea where he is, but knowing I need my brother.

Growing up, I was always the closest to Kol. He was my confidant, and now I need him to tell me that this pain won't last forever, lest I do something stupid.

"Kol!"

The sconces flicker in the dim hallways while I charge down them but settle when Kol steps out of his bedroom wearing only dark pajama pants. I probably interrupted him and Rapsody.

I cringe. It's just a reminder of what I'll never have again with Ariana.

"What the hell is going on?" he says, moving toward me, his expression a mix of anger and concern.

Now that I've found him, it's as though I can't push the words past my throat. It feels tight, and my breathing comes out wheezy.

"Hey, hey, hey." Kol clamps me on the shoulder. "Relax. Breathe." He pulls me into one of the sitting rooms. "Here, sit down." He forces me into one of the chairs. "Now count with me and breathe."

He leads me through a breathing exercise, and eventually the tightness in my throat relaxes, and I'm able to breathe.

"I don't know what that was." My voice is hoarse.

Kol sits across from me. "Could have been the start of a panic attack. Rapsody used to get them sometimes. Reminded me of that."

Unbelievable. This woman and her lies will be my end.

I close my eyes, remembering the words Ariana just spoke to me. They were like an arrow and my heart was her bull's-eye, leaving it a bloody pulp mess.

"What happened?" Kol asks, voice grave.

"She lied. She's been lying this whole time." I push both hands through my hair and rest my elbows on my knees, staring at the carpet.

"Who? Ariana?"

I nod, unable to say her name.

"What did she lie about?"

Her feelings for me. That she loved me.

I don't admit that out loud. "She's a con. She's been stealing from us."

Kol looks at me in confusion, and I bolt up out of my seat to pace.

"The first lie was when she showed up. She didn't tell me she was the one who saved me on the beach."

Kol blinks a few times. "Wait... *she* saved your life? What about this Leah person who's been staying here?"

I shake my head. "Everything's a lie."

"Sid, you're not making sense."

Ariana was the one who saved me. Did she know that I'd been apathetically trying to take my own life that day? Had she known when she showed up and used that information to manipulate me? If she knew I was trying to end my life, she knew I was lost and broken and that made me an easy mark.

The pain in my stomach makes me bend over with a hand pressed to it. God, to think that she may have known all along feels like another sort of betrayal.

"Fuck!" I stand and shout at the ceiling.

"Calm down. Start from the beginning and tell me what's going on."

So I do. I manage to get my thoughts together long enough to explain the sordid story to him.

When I'm finished, he flops back in the chair and blows out a long breath. "What a mess."

Unshed tears burn in my eyes. "I was an idiot for ever thinking someone could love me like that."

"Sid, I saw you guys together. She may have lied about—"

"I don't want to hear it!" I shout.

My cell phone rings from the inside pocket of my suit, but I ignore it. When it starts up again, I pull it out to see who it is.

"It's Ash." I toss the phone to Kol. I don't want to talk to my big brother right now.

Kol swipes the screen to take the call. "Yeah?" His gaze flicks over to me. "Yeah, he's here. Sure, we'll meet you there in a minute."

I groan. "What the hell does he need us for this late at night?" It's well past business hours.

"Two men just showed up at the gate saying they're Ariana's father and brother. Wouldn't leave. Insisted that they need to see her. Said she's not answering her phone." My face transforms into a scowl as Kol stands from the chair. "Let's go."

"What the fuck are they doing here?"

He shrugs as we make our way out of the room toward the communal part of the house. "Who knows, but let's try to figure it out. Try to keep your shit together."

I want to say fuck off, but somehow, I keep my mouth shut. Kol leads us to one of the living areas in the main part of the house, and I see the guy I saw Ariana at the bar with, her "brother" Bastion, and another man who's probably in his late forties.

The moment I see him, I want to shove my fist through his face for what he did to his daughter, how he raised her by using her in his cons. Maybe if he hadn't, she wouldn't have tuned out to be such a fucking liar and what we had would have been real.

But it looks as though someone beat me to it. Both men have obviously been worked over. Between them, they have bruises on their faces, a swollen lip, and a cut on the forehead. That at least brings me some level of satisfaction.

Asher looks between Kol and me, obviously sensing that something is off. "What's going on?"

Kol nods for Asher to join him on the other side of the massive room, and the two of them walk over there, leaving me with the two pieces of shit.

"What the hell do you two want?" I say.

"We need to see Ariana," Bastion says, then looks nervously between his father and me.

"Why?" My head tilts in a move akin to a predator assessing its prey.

"Family emergency," her father says.

My eyes narrow on him. As my mom predicted, I am the wolf stalking its prey. "Got another con job for her to run for you?"

The shock on his face almost makes me laugh. Almost.

"What are... that's ridiculous," he says, attempting to look as if I've offended him.

"I know all about how you raised your daughter and son." I flick my hand in Bastion's direction. "What kind of father does that? Makes her think her worth is in how well she can screw people over. Sells her off to the highest bidder when she gets older. You're a disgusting piece of shit, and if it weren't for you, maybe she wouldn't be the liar and con that she is."

Kol must be done filling Asher in because the two of them join us, standing by my side.

Bastion stands from the couch, hands raised in the universal sign for surrender. "She's obviously told you everything. But you should know, she wanted nothing to do with our way of life anymore. Was working two jobs to try to make a living because she wanted so badly to be done with it all. It wasn't until he got mixed up with Uma that she was forced to participate again because Uma threatened all of our lives."

At least her father has the decency to look somewhat ashamed.

"I don't give a shit. None of that matters. Explain what you're doing here." I set my hands on my hips.

Her father stands. "We're afraid that Uma—the woman I owe money to—might try to hurt her. She's become more unhinged."

The hairs on the back of my neck stand on end. "What do you mean?"

"This is courtesy of her and her goons." Bastion points at his face. "Most people would be happy we were coming up with the money to pay her off, but every time I showed up with a chunk of change to put toward the debt, she seemed more and more agitated. Wanted to know how we were coming up with the money, but I never told her."

That makes no sense.

"A few days ago her goons picked us up and beat the shit out of us until we told them," her dad says.

"I tried contacting her to give her a heads-up as soon as they let us go, but she hasn't answered my calls or texts," Bastion says.

I think back. Ariana has had her phone on her at all times. I've seen her using it, and she hasn't been sending any calls to voicemail.

Bastion must see my thoughts on my face. "She had another phone she was using to contact me." He cringes.

My hands drop from my hips and fist at my sides. "Why do you think she'd want to hurt Ariana?"

"One of her guys was talking about how Uma was pissed we were probably going to be able to pay off the loan. She'd wanted to use it as leverage to force Ariana to work for her."

"Ari's got the gift. Uma could see it, too," her dad says like a proud father.

I scowl. "Uma's here."

Their expressions drop, eyes wide, panic slowly masking their faces.

Bastion steps forward. "What do you mean she's here?"

The panic in his voice causes my pulse to spike. "She showed up a few days ago. Said her name was Leah and claimed to be the one who saved me from drowning a few months back."

"Ari's the one who saved you," Bastion sneers.

I step toward him until we're almost nose to nose, and it's all I can do not to pummel them both into the ground. "I didn't know any of this until a short time ago. Only you two and Ariana knew about the deception you were running."

"If Uma's here, then Ari's in danger. Where is she?" her dad snaps.

The words "Ari's in danger" snap me out of my rage and thirst for retaliation. I blink several times.

A feeling worse than when I found out she betrayed me moves through my veins like sludge. I cannot let anything happen to her, no matter how complicated my feelings are for her.

"She's in the east wing." I run from the room and hear footsteps behind me, but I don't bother to stop and see who might be following.

I have to get to Ariana and make sure she's okay.

CHAPTER

THIRTY-FOUR

ARIANA

My cheeks sting from all my saltwater tears, and my chest aches. The look of utter devastation on Obsidian's face when he figured out I had betrayed him will never leave me.

What hurts the most is that he believes that me loving him was all part of some plan. He doubts my feelings for him are real. It reminds me of the broken man I first met who thought he wasn't deserving of love.

Maybe in time, he'll understand that I do love him. I know he'll never forgive me or give me another chance, but I need him to know it was all real.

A knock at my bedroom door causes hope to soar. Maybe he's cooled off and is ready to talk to me. He could just as well be here to tell me to gather my things and leave though.

I swing open the door, and Uma bursts into the room. I slam the door behind her and spin to face her. All of my anger and frustration at my powerlessness where she's concerned comes to the forefront. "What do you want?"

She has that stupid caustic grin as she always does. "I came to make you an offer."

I fold my arms. "What kind of offer?"

The only thing I want from her is for her to leave and to forgive my dad's debts.

"Come work for me, and I'll wipe your dad's debt clean."

My mouth drops open. "Is that what this is all about? Is that why you showed up here?"

"Think of what we could accomplish together. I've been watching you for years, Ariana. You're very talented. Innocent enough for people to never suspect you, but devious enough to get the job done."

I drop my hands to my sides and step toward her. "I already told you. I'm not interested in living the life of a criminal anymore. Once you're paid off, I'm done."

Her laugh sends ripples of discomfort up my spine. "You're never going to get that debt paid off. The clock is ticking, and time is running out. Especially now that you'll no longer steal from your lover."

My lips press together into a thin line.

"Yes, that's right," she says. "I figured it out. I had my suspicions before I got here, but once I saw you and Obsidian together, it cemented it for me. The reason why your brother had been empty-handed the past couple of weeks."

Fuck this bitch. "You never said how you even found out where I was."

Another smirk. "We beat the information of your father and brother."

My stomach drops like dead weight. "Are they okay?"

"Of course they are. I wouldn't kill them—yet. They're too easy to use as motivation for you."

"Leave them alone!"

She shrugs. "Sure. All you have to do is agree to come work for me."

I step forward. "I'm never going to work for you. What don't you understand about that? My conscience is not for sale."

"Just your cunt is?" She arches an eyebrow. "Is that why you spread your legs for your billionaire boss?"

I hate the way she's cheapening what Obsidian and I share —or shared. God, I'm not sure I'll survive this heartbreak if Obsidian doesn't forgive me.

"You need to leave. I'm not going to come work for you, and we *will* get that loan paid off in time."

"Are you sure about that, Ariana? Every choice has consequences. You might not like the consequences of this one."

I stab a finger in her direction. "I'm sure that I'm never going to work for someone like you. I'd rather die first."

Her head tilts. "That can be arranged."

The first fission of real fear ripples through my body. I attempt to call her bluff. "You're not going to kill me here. In this house."

One corner of her lips tilts up in a sadistic smile. "Maybe I will. Maybe I'll say you shot yourself after losing the love of your life." When I blanch, she laughs. "Oh, yes, sweetie, it's written all over your face. Either you confessed out of guilt, or he found out somehow. In your deep sorrow and regret, you shot yourself. Once you're out of the picture, maybe I can have my turn with him."

She licks her lips, and the thought of that mouth being anywhere near Obsidian fuels a rage so powerful that I feel as though I could whirl into my own tornado. I charge at her with a scream, but she's ready for me and sends me flying to the side into a piece of furniture. The air is knocked from my lungs, and I gasp, clutching my throat.

Uma picks me up by the hair and drags me over to the desk and chair set against one wall. I try to fight her off, but it's nearly impossible when I struggle to breathe. My panic rises the longer I can't get a deep breath, but eventually I'm able to inhale a small amount.

She gets me in the chair, and man, she came prepared. I kick and scream, flailing as she ties one of my hands to the armrest. I fight against her, kicking with my legs and reaching out with my one free hand. My nails rake down her face and snag on her necklace—my mother's necklace. It snaps and pearls scatter, pinging around the floor around my feet.

She groans a frustrated sigh and yanks my other hand

down. She's stronger than me, and she ties to the other armrest.

Shit. Shit. Shit.

I will not die like this. I can't. I still have to make everything better with Obsidian. I have to let him know I love him. If he thinks I killed myself, he'll never be able to live with the guilt.

Uma pulls a gun from the back waistband of her pants and aims it at me. "God, I want to fuck you up, but I can't if I want everyone to believe you killed yourself. Having your face full of fresh bruises would be hard to explain."

I try to stand, but the wooden chair is too heavy. A scream rips from my throat at the pain in my ribs. Attempting to work my hands free, I wiggle them around, biting the inside of my mouth until I taste copper.

She raises the gun. Knowing she has to get close to me if she's going to try to mask my death as a suicide, I kick and scream as soon as she's near enough, hoping someone will hear me. My foot connects with her hand holding the gun, and it slides across the floor, close to the wall. She shouts in frustration and backtracks to the gun.

Glancing around feverishly, panicking that my time is drawing short, and I'm not sure what else to do, I scream, "Help! Help!"

"You're gonna regret that, bitch." When she turns around with the gun in her hand, she's clearly changed her mind about making it look like a suicide. I've pushed her to a breaking point where she doesn't care.

I close my eyes and wait for death to come. My only regret is not telling Obsidian that I love him one last time. I hope he finds peace.

CHAPTER

THIRTY-FIVE

I reach the east wing in record time, racing down the hall and peeking into every room I pass, hoping to find Ariana. A scream echoes from the direction of her bedroom, and I sprint there, finding the door shut and locked.

I hear the commotion inside and consider my options. I want to pound on the door, but if Uma is in there, and she knows I'm frantic to get Ariana, I give her the advantage.

Ariana's father and brother arrive seconds later. I don't know where Kol and Asher are. Her dad goes to open the door, and I push him back.

"If Uma has a gun, and we tell her we're here, you're an easy shot. I can get in a different way and use the element of surprise. You stay here. Got it?"

It takes him a second of disagreeing with me, but eventually her dad nods then Bastion nods.

"Good. You hear shots of any kind though, you break down that door. We clear?"

When they both nod again, I don't bother wasting any more time before I run to my bedroom.

As soon as I'm inside the master suite, I head to the bookcase and pull the Poe book to reveal the entrance to the secret passageway. The dark tunnel feels so much longer than every night I've sneaked into Ariana's room.

So much could go wrong here.

If Uma's facing the secret door, she may see me, and I won't be able to get the jump on her. What if she's already hurt Ariana? What if I'm too late?

I push all the what-ifs from my mind.

Through the door, it's difficult to hear what's going on in there, but I hear some kind of muffled altercation. Though it spikes my adrenaline further, at least I hear two voices so I know Ariana is still alive.

Slowly, way slower than I'd like, I slide open the portion of the wall just a crack to reveal Ariana's bedroom. My heart seizes when I see her tied to a chair, struggling uselessly to free herself. Closer to me, Uma's reaching to grab a gun off the floor. When she has it in hand, she turns her back to me, pointing the gun at Ariana.

"You're gonna regret that, bitch," Uma sneers.

"Help me, someone!" Ariana screams.

The panic in her voice and her eyes is almost my undoing. I don't have a gun on me or anything to go up against Uma, but it doesn't matter. I will gut that fucking bitch if she harms a hair on Ariana's head.

Before I can decide the best course of action, the door to the bedroom bursts open and Ariana's father rushes through. Uma shifts her stance and fires behind Ariana, hitting him. His body sinks to the floor.

There's no time to waste. I push the secret door open fully and rip the lamp from the bedside table where it sits, yanking the cord out of the wall, and swing it toward Uma's head. She's halfway turned to me with the gun raised when there's a sickening crunch as the lamp hits her skull, and she falls to the floor. A gush of blood rushes from her head.

Her eyes stare ahead, unseeing, and she doesn't move. I step around her and kick the gun from her hand, then I whip around to face Ariana. Tears streak down her cheeks and relief floods her face.

I rush over to her and undo the binds holding her to the chair. "Are you okay? Are you hurt?" My eyes scan her from head to toe. Besides some red marks on her wrists, I don't see anything.

"My dad," she says in a broken voice.

Hesitating, I leave her and crouch beside him. Blood rushes from the wound in his shoulder.

"Get me something to press down on this wound." I check for a pulse, and I'm relieved to find one. Relieved not because I give a shit whether this guy lives or dies after the predicament he put Ariana in, but because I know she'd grieve his loss.

Ariana returns seconds later with a shirt, and I notice she winces a bit when she bends to pass it to me. I ball up the shirt and push it down on the wound. Before I can ask her where she's in pain, Kol and Bastion rush into the room.

"What the hell happened?" Kol asks, gun in hand.

"Uma's dead. This one burst through the door, making himself an easy target even though I told him not to." I turn my attention to Bastion. "What the hell were you thinking, letting him go inside?"

Bastion glares at me. "When he heard Ari shouting for help, there was no stopping him. I tried. After I heard the shot, I ran to get help and found him." He points at Kol.

"Ash is meeting with the authorities at the front and will lead them back here."

I nod.

"Ari, are you okay?" Bastion asks, rushing over to her and pulling her into a hug.

She sucks in a sharp breath in his hold.

"Careful, she's hurt," I snap.

He pulls away, and his eyes run over her body. "What's wrong?"

"She threw me down," Ariana says. "I think I hurt my ribs or something."

My teeth snap together when I think of the pain she's in.

"How is he?" she asks.

I look up and see deep concern in her eyes. "He should be fine as long as he gets to the hospital soon."

She nods and looks at me as though she wants to say something more, but she doesn't.

I hate the distance between us. It doesn't feel right. But what else am I supposed to do after what she did?

A few minutes later, paramedics arrive and take her father out on a gurney. It's clear to me that Ariana is torn between going with her father and staying with me.

I nod after the paramedics. "Go. You need to get checked out too."

Her shoulders sag as she walks out with a paramedic.

Whatever. I need to clear my head after everything that's gone down tonight. It's been a fucking *lot*.

Kol and Asher stand on either side of me, watching her go.

The police arrive, and we give them a quick rundown of what happened. Asher, being Asher, manages to put them off for a bit, allowing them to do what they need to in order to process the room, but tells them that if they'd like to speak with us further, they'll need to talk to our lawyers.

"You okay?" Kol asks with a frown.

"What do you think?"

"I think we could all use a drink," Asher says. "Let's head to my office before the authorities want to speak with us all. We can have some of my Macallan. I'll text Nero to join us."

I nod, and the three of us walk to the west wing and sit in

Asher's office. He's just handed Kol and me each a glass of whiskey when Nero walks in.

"What the hell is going on?" Nero asks.

I fill them all in, starting with what Marcel told me and ending with what happened in Ariana's room.

"There has been way too much shit going on with this family the past couple of years," Nero says.

I bring the glass to my lips and down all the scotch, then hold out the empty glass toward Asher for a refill. With a sigh, he gets out of the chair, takes my glass, and brings it back half full. I immediately take another healthy sip.

We're all quiet for a minute, my brothers staring at me.

Kol says, "What are you going to do about Ariana?"

I give him a what-the-fuck look. "What choice do I have but to pack her things and kick her out?"

"There's always a choice," Asher says.

I look at him incredulously. I did not expect him, of all people, to suggest I should give Ariana another chance.

He shrugs. "From what you've said, she grew up in a shit situation. We know better than anyone what that's like and how it can affect you."

My mood darkens further at the allusion to our father and the hell he put us all through.

"She only did what she did because she was desperate to save her family and herself, Sid. If it were you, you'd do anything in your power to protect the people you love. You have. We *all* have."

I stiffen, knowing Asher's referring to the night our father died. "That doesn't mean I can forgive her for deceiving me for so long. How do I know what she said she felt for me is real? Maybe it was just a ploy to make it easier to steal shit under my nose."

Kol shrugs. "Maybe. But you won't know unless you talk to her."

"It wasn't a ploy," Nero says.

I whip my head in his direction.

"I've seen you two together, and there's no way she was faking that," Nero adds. "She's in love with you, Sid."

Looking away from him, I stare into the amber liquid in my glass.

"I know you think you don't deserve it, but you do. She looks at you like Rapsody does me, Cinder looks at Nero, and for some reason, the way Anabelle looks at Asher," Kol says.

"Fuck off," Asher says. "By some miracle, the universe gifted us each with the perfect woman. Don't let her slip through your fingers because she was up against the wall and had to do what she had to do for her family. I'm not saying you don't question her about it, and it might take time, but you guys can get past this. We'd do just about anything for our family, right?"

"If I know you, you've been waiting for the shit to hit the fan since you realized you were in love with her." Kol gives me a look daring me to say he's wrong.

But I can't. I was so happy with her, but that feeling of dread still seeped in, telling me it would all end soon enough. That our time would come to an end. That I'd never be able to keep something so good in my life.

"How did you forgive Cinder when you found out she lied to you about Maude?" I ask Nero.

He shrugs. "It was easy. When her life was in danger, it became clear to me that I still loved her. I would've done anything to save her. Anything. That right there told me what I needed to know."

"When you saw that Uma had a gun on Ariana, how did you feel, Sid?" Kol asks.

I sigh into my glass. "Like my life would be over if hers was."

"That's your answer," Kol says in a grave voice.

"It's just a choice, Sid. It's a decision to forgive her, then you move on," Nero adds.

I suck in a breath and toss back the rest of my drink. Could it really be that easy? Just decide to forgive Ariana and start fresh?

"I'll think about it," I mutter, setting my empty glass on the coffee table and standing to leave.

I need to be by myself to think, and I know exactly where I'm going to do it—the secret garden.

THIRTY-SIX

ARIANA

Hours later, I step into the hospital room where my dad is sleeping. He had to undergo surgery to repair the damage caused by the bullet, but he'll be fine.

I had to have X-rays done, and they wanted to make sure I didn't have a concussion. None of my ribs are broken, just badly bruised, and it hurts to move, but I'm alive and that's what matters. Everyone who matters is alive.

The cops wanted to speak with me after all my tests were done. I spoke to them because I didn't think I could put them off, but the whole time, I just wanted to lay eyes on my father and see for myself that he's all right. Some of the tension leaves my body when I see his chest moving up and down in slumber.

Bastion sits in a chair in the corner of the room, but stands when I walk in. "You get checked out? Everything okay?"

"Yeah, my ribs are bruised. Fine beyond that. How's Dad?"

We both look at him.

"Should wake up soon. Surgery went well, and he should be fine after some rehab."

I nod, the full brunt of everything that's happened in the last twelve hours hitting me full force, and I wobble on my feet.

"Here, sit." He helps me over to the chair he vacated. "Did the police already talk to you?"

I nod. "You?"

He frowns. "Yeah."

"So much for staying off the cops' radar," I say with no humor in my voice.

"What do you think will happen?" Bastion asks. "You think that boyfriend of yours will use his influence to make any repercussions disappear?"

The mention of Obsidian makes my chest ache more than my ribs. "He's not my boyfriend. At least not anymore."

"Ari."

Something in Bastion's tone causes me to look at him.

"I saw that man when he thought something was going to happen to you, and I'm telling you, he hasn't written you off."

His words plant a small seed of hope inside me, but I push the feeling down, unwilling to believe that Obsidian could ever move forward with me. I saw the devastation on his face when he learned the truth about me. There's no coming back from that.

"We'll see," I say to put Bastion off the subject.

"I know I told you a man like him wouldn't go for a woman like you, but I was wrong. When I got on the plane, I regretted telling you that. It's hard to see the world differently from the one we were raised in. I think I got kind of jealous that you'd get out and have an amazing life, and I'd be banded with Dad forever. But Obsidian should forgive you because you're too good for him."

A smile tips my lips.

"You're good for one another. Love and all that shit, you know."

I laugh. "Thanks, Bastion."

"And if he doesn't forgive you, find another lucky billionaire bastard."

I grab his hand and squeeze. "Thanks."

Dad groans, and his eyes flutter.

I tense and cringe when the stabbing pain in my ribs hits me again. "Dad?"

His head moves side to side, then his eyes open. It takes a moment for him to focus, but when he does, a small smile tilts his lips.

"Kids..." His voice is hoarse.

"Do you want some water, Dad?"

"Nah." He tries to wave me off then flinches.

Tears well in my eyes. Not only did he rush in and put himself in danger to help me, but if that bullet had been a few inches either way, there's a good chance he wouldn't be alive.

"You okay?" he asks me.

"Fine." I nod.

He looks at Bastion standing behind me. "Uma?"

"Dead. Obsidian killed her."

My shoulders sink. I can't help but wonder how Obsidian feels about that. I made him a murderer.

"Good. That's good." My dad looks down at his body, then turns his gaze back to me. "Ari... I don't know what to say." He swallows hard. "I owe you an apology."

"It's okay, Dad."

He shakes his head. "No, it's not. I put you in harm's way. If Uma had killed you, I don't know how I ever would've lived with myself. But I owe you an apology for more than just that. Your boyfriend was right to come at me for how you were raised. It wasn't right. I just... after your mom left, I didn't know how I was gonna support you except to do it the only way I knew how. But I never should've dragged you into it."

I swallow past the painful lump in my throat. "I know you did your best." I grab his hand, fighting against the pain in my ribs. "But I don't want anything to do with that life anymore. And I really hope that after this, you don't either."

He sniffles and blinks the tears out of his eyes. "I'm gonna give it a go. I can't promise you I'll be perfect, but I'll try."

Knowing that's the best I'm ever going to get from him, I nod and squeeze his hand. "Deal."

I stay for a while longer, until I can barely keep my eyes open. My father has long since gone back to sleep, leaving Bastion and me in quiet of just the beeping hospital equipment.

"I need some sleep. What are you going to do?" I ask.

Bastion shrugs. "Probably just sleep here in this chair. You should go back to the manor and sleep. We can catch up with each other tomorrow and figure everything out."

I nod, dreading returning to the manor. But I have nowhere else to go and all my things are there. If security won't let me through the front gates when I arrive, I'll come back here.

THE NEXT MORNING, I shift and the pain of my ribs makes me groan. My eyes slowly open, and I yelp, sliding back in the bed. I place my hand over my ribs. "Shit."

Obsidian sits in a chair in the corner of the room Marcel showed me to last night. I was surprised when I arrived at Midnight Manor, and my things weren't waiting for me in garbage bags outside the front door. There was no way I was going to be able to sleep in my old room though, so I breathed a sigh of relief when Marcel led me here.

"Hey," I say.

He rises off the chair and stalks toward the bed, his dark gaze never leaving me. I shift to sit up, but grunt in pain from the stabbing pain in my ribs.

Obsidian raises his hand. "Stay where you are. Marcel tells me you have some pretty badly bruised ribs."

I didn't realize when Marcel was asking me questions last night that it was for Obsidian's benefit.

"Could be worse... if you hadn't intervened. Thank you." My eyes sting, but I hold the tears at bay.

"You don't need to thank me, Ariana. Regardless of what went down before, I still wouldn't let anyone hurt you."

It's just because he's a good man, despite what he may think. Don't read into it.

"Either way, I appreciate it. You probably saved my dad too, so thank you."

He nods, lips pressed together. "I want you to know that I talked to the police, and they won't need to talk to you, your brother or your dad again. They determined that I acted in self-defense and won't be looking into last night further."

"Thank you," I say in a small voice.

I know for certain he or his brothers have used their influence, or money, to make it go away. After what I did to them, I certainly didn't expect their help.

"I want to talk to you about why you were here."

"Obsidian, I—"

He raises his hand and sits on the side of the bed. "I've been thinking about it all night." He pauses, and I wait for him to continue. "I understand why you did it. I've done worse to protect the people I care most about, believe me." He blows out a breath and pushes a hand through his hair. "I don't like it—obviously. But I understand it. I would have done the same. We didn't know each other when you first came here, and reflecting back, I see now the times when you seemed conflicted about something, but I couldn't put my finger on it."

I breathe shakily, unable to believe what he's saying. "The closer we got, the more I despised myself. I couldn't even take anything the last couple of times I met my brother."

He sighs, and his eyes grow kinder. "Your brother told me that months before you even got here, you opted out of the family business. That you wanted nothing more to do with it."

I nod fast a few times. "That's true. It never really felt right to me, but as I got into my twenties, I found it harder and harder to live with myself. After we ran a scam, all I could think about was how the people we'd targeted would recover. How long would it take them to make that money back? How untrusting would they be going through life now? Would they go into a depression and commit suicide? I just didn't want any part of it any longer."

He must hear the truth in my words because he gently takes my hand. "I believe you. And I believe that you're still the same woman I fell in love with. It might take me some time to fully get back to where we were, but I'd like to try."

Elation fills me like helium to a balloon, so fast I fear I might bust. He's going to give me a second chance? The emotion is too much to contain, and I burst into tears.

"I never thought I'd get the chance to make this up to you." I cringe from the pain crying creates in my ribs.

"Shhh. Careful, don't hurt yourself." He thumbs the tears off my cheeks. "It's going to be okay. *We're* going to be okay."

Neither of us knows the future, but I'll do everything in my power to prove to him that everything we had is the real deal. We're the lucky ones who found true love.

EPILOGUE

OBSIDIAN

It didn't take more than a few weeks for things to return to normal between Ariana and me. Basically, as her ribs healed, so did the fractured relationship between us.

She opened up about her past in a way she hadn't before. Since I already knew how she'd been raised, it seemed easy for her to tell me about the scams her dad had both his kids run, the rules he set in place to make sure they never got caught, and how they moved around a lot so that they'd never be discovered.

While I was living in my own kind of hell with my father, so was she. Different, but no less difficult.

Knowing about her past actually brought us closer.

Her father and brother returned to the West Coast as soon as her father was discharged from the hospital. I offered to fly us out there if she wanted to spend some time by his side, but Ariana said she needed some distance from them both. That she loved them and always would, but at the moment, she wanted to concentrate on me, on us.

Sometimes when she says things like that, it takes me aback that anyone could care about me so much. Decades spent thinking I'm worthless and so much like my father that I'm undeserving of love are hard to undo, but I'm slowly unraveling those knots.

The only thing left to take care of was Brandon. Ariana never brought him up again, but I hadn't forgotten about him. Not at all. Which is why Brandon found himself the victim of a hit and run accident that will leave him in the hospital and doing rehab for months. It was less pain than I wanted to inflict on that sack of shit, but anything more and it might get back to Ariana.

We're in my bedroom—our bedroom now—still gathering our breath after making love. I think we make love more than fuck these days. I never would've believed it, but in a lot of ways, it's more fulfilling. It doesn't mean she's not still my good girl though.

Nero was right about forgiveness being a decision. And once I'd made the decision to forgive her, I knew quickly that I'd already made another decision.

I decided that I don't want to waste any more time. I know how I feel about her and how she feels about me. Why wait any longer to begin our lives together? I want to be able to call Ariana my wife.

I roll toward the nightstand and pull open the top drawer, rummaging around inside for the ring box. I've had it for a couple of weeks, but I wasn't sure how I wanted to propose.

I didn't want to do some big grand gesture—and maybe that will turn out to be a mistake—but I wanted to do it when the time felt right. Which is now.

"What are you looking for?" she asks with humor in her voice.

With my back to her, I open the ring box and pull out the ring.

Choosing the ring turned out to be way more stressful than I would have thought. Especially because money was no object. I can buy Ariana literally any ring I want, which meant every option was available to me.

But when I spoke to the jeweler and told him what Ariana is like, he came up with a few sketches, and this one was perfect. It has a large pearl in the center with diamonds surrounding it in a design that almost makes it look like a star. It's different and a little art deco looking, and god, I hope she loves it.

I roll over to face her with the ring clutched between my thumb and forefinger.

The smile falls from Ariana's face, and she gasps, looking from the ring to me and back several times.

"Ariana, I am so deeply and firmly entrenched in our love. I cannot imagine moving forward in the world without you by my side. I wouldn't even consider it living because you're the one who breathed life into me. You are the one who made me feel like I had something to offer someone else. You are the woman I want to spend the rest of my life trying to make happy. Will you do me the great honor of becoming my wife?"

It probably only takes her a few seconds to answer, but I swear it feels like minutes. All I can hear is the thrumming of my heart and the whooshing of the blood flowing through my veins.

Then a smile breaks out on her face, and she practically tackles me, kissing my face and rolling so that her naked body is on top of mine. Of course, my dick notices, regardless of the moment, and it hardens underneath her.

Ariana's kissing my face all over, and a laugh breaks loose from my throat. "Does that mean yes?"

"Yes, Obsidian! Nothing would make me happier than being your wife. Absolutely nothing." She presses her lips to mine.

The kiss deepens as we both throw all the emotion we're feeling in this moment into it. She shifts her hips, and I slip inside her from below. Then she moans and moves over me. And I take her left hand and slide the ring onto her finger.

"You're never taking this off," I tell her.

"Never," she agrees.

IT TAKES hours for us to make our way out of bed, but Ariana insists that we make it to dinner with everyone so that we can announce our engagement. She's excited to tell the girls, who she's become closer to since everything went down.

It's a funny thing. People are always afraid of their twisted truths coming out, but once they do, the secrets lose their power over you.

I'm sliding on my shoes in my walk-in closet when I hear Ariana say from the bedroom, "Obsidian, did you bring this down from your treasure trove?"

I step out of the closet to see what she's talking about and find her standing by the dresser, holding the jar of sand from the last vacation my brothers and I ever took with our mom.

Forehead wrinkled, I walk toward her. "No, I haven't touched it. How the hell did it get in here?"

"Are you just messing with me?" she asks, putting it down.

I raise both hands. "I swear. I haven't touched it since that night in the tower." She looks a little shell-shocked, and I step forward and grip her shoulders. "Ariana, what is it? What has you so freaked out?"

"I... I never told you this, and please don't think I'm crazy, but... the night I first found you in the secret garden, I woke up and saw a trail of sand from my bed leading to the bedroom door. I followed it there, and the trail kept going, and so I followed it, and it led me to find you in the garden. The same thing happened the night I found you up in the turret. Both times when I woke up, it just felt like I was *supposed* to follow the trail wherever it led. I don't think I could have ignored it if I tried."

I blink a few times.

"You think I'm nuts."

Shaking my head, I squeeze her shoulders. "No, not at all." I look at the jar of sand, still wondering how it got here and wondering if it could really be true. "I think maybe my mom was helping us along."

A warm, soft smile transforms her face. She wraps her arms around me and squeezes me tightly. "I like the idea of that."

"Me too."

We stay in that embrace for longer than usual, and when we separate, we leave the bedroom hand in hand. As we make our way through the manor to the patio where dinner will be served tonight—since it's still warm out in the evenings—I realize that something about the house feels... different. Like the air isn't so thick, the shadows not so pronounced.

Maybe there is a way to change the legacy of Midnight Manor. Maybe it starts with love.

When we arrive on the patio, everyone else is already there, standing with a drink in hand, mingling.

"Hey, guys," Anabelle says.

Ariana raises her hand in greeting. "Hi, sorry we're a little late."

That's all it takes for Cinder to notice the new piece of jewelry on Ariana's hand. "Holy shit."

"What?" Rapsody looks between Cinder and Ariana with concern and confusion. I see when she notices the ring too because her face relaxes, and she squeals.

Next is Anabelle, who shouts, "Congratulations," and rushes over to give Ariana a hug.

My brothers still look confused, so I do them a favor and say, "Ariana and I just got engaged."

Each one of them smiles, their faces filled with more than happiness. It's the satisfaction that despite what went on in this house for so many years, all four of us came through and managed to find our own happiness, regardless of how difficult our dad tried to make that for us.

They each hug me, offering me their best wishes, then turn their attention to their future sister-in-law, who is still showing the girls her ring.

I watch my brothers and their significant others interact with Ariana and offer their congratulations, knowing I'm no longer on the outside. I too know what it means to love and be loved in return. And despite the hell it took to get here, I wouldn't have it any other way.

Ariana glances over her shoulder and smiles.

My angel. My savior. Soon to be my wife.

The End

IF YOU WANT MORE dark and sexy books from P. Rayne, be sure to check out Vow of Revenge, the first installment of The Mafia Academy Series—a dark romance set at a boarding school for the sons and daughters of the most powerful mafia lords.

ALSO BY P. RAYNE

Mafia Academy

Vow of Revenge

Corrupting the Innocent

Corrupting the Mafia King's Sister

Craving My Rival

Standalones

Beautifully Scarred

Midnight Manor

Moonlit Thorns

Shattered Vows

Midnight Whispers

Twisted Truths

ACKNOWLEDGMENTS

We're sad to see this series come to an end. It was a blast to write from start to finish and we had so much fun delving in and discovering what makes each of the brother's tick because they're all so different.

Full disclosure—this reimagining was originally going to be Little Red Riding Hood, as some of you might have guessed from the wolf tattoo. LOL But as the series progressed, we felt more and more like that just didn't fit. Not only with Obsidian's character but also in the storyline. We didn't have a deep burning need to tell a Little Red Riding Hood reimaging and when we went to plot it out, it just wasn't working, which is where The Little Mermaid came in. We had a spark of an idea, and it snowballed from there.

We loved the idea of having BOTH characters appear to be one thing but be hiding something underneath. Ariana presents as a pretty, sweet, innocent girl who hides her history as a grifter and criminal. Obsidian is suave and debonair to most, but he hides his ugly history and some... proclivities, shall we say?

Sid felt so undeserving of the love Ariana wanted to give him, and we're a sucker for a hero who finds himself unworthy of his lady love, only for him to discover that he had it in him all along to be the man she needed.

Even though the series is complete, Midnight Manor still has its secrets, as you well know. We know you're wondering why we didn't delve into what happened the night Ramsey Voss was killed. That was intentional. We'll leave it up to your imagination as to what you think happened, and maybe someday all will be revealed, but for now, the Voss brothers still hold that secret close to their chests. That said, we'd love to hear any theories you might have.

We have to give a huge thanks to everyone who helped bring this book to market...

A big shout to Regina Wamba for another gorgeous cover. Her work on the entire Midnight Manor series is truly a work of art and we're so pleased with how the series turned out.

Thanks as always to Cassie at Joy editing for the line edits and for My Brother's Editor for the proofreading. You both helped make this story what it is today.

The Valentine PR crew always keeps us in check and follows up to make sure we're hitting those deadlines. Not only do we need it, but we appreciate it!

A HUGE hug to every blogger, influencer and reader who has supported this series! We genuinely appreciate every review, edit, recommendation to your reader friends, rating, and social media shout-out you give us. We see you and are so, so grateful! <3 Word of mouth is truly the best way to try and gain traction on a new series and we appreciate everyone who has advocated to their reader buddies to pick up this series.

And of course, a massive thanks to YOU for picking this story and making it all the way to the end. We appreciate you spending your precious time in the world of Midnight Manor.

For now, we're finished in this world and our attention will turn to the bookstore releases of the Mafia Academy series, which we are so, so excited for. It's truly a dream come true for us both! If you like the sound of a secretive, private college where only the sons and daughters of the mafia can attend, be sure to check it out! After that, we'll be back with a new world for you to escape into!

xo,

Piper & Rayne

ABOUT P. RAYNE

P. Rayne is the pseudonym for the darker side of the USA Today Bestselling Author duo, Piper Rayne. Under P. Rayne you'll find dark, forbidden and sexy romances.